First Language Lessons

for the Well-Trained Mind

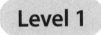

Level 1

by Jessie Wise

Peace Hill Press
www.peacehillpress.com

Publisher's Cataloging-In-Publication Data

(Prepared by The Donohue Group, Inc.)

Wise, Jessie.
  First language lessons for the well-trained mind. Level 1 / by Jessie Wise.

     p. : ill. ; cm.

     Includes index.
     ISBN: 978-1-933339-44-3

  1. English language--Grammar--Study and teaching (Primary) 2. English language-
  -Composition and exercises--Study and teaching (Primary) 3. Language arts
  (Primary) I. Title.

  LB1528 .W573 2010
  372.61   2010921160

For children everywhere—
and for my grandchildren especially

TABLE OF CONTENTS

Acknowledgments

I am grateful to my daughter, Susan Wise Bauer, for giving me a vision for this book, and then sharing her time, computer expertise, and research experience to make it a reality.

I am indebted to Sara Buffington for her editing work polishing the many revisions of the manuscript, for her contributions of poetry and prose, and for her adapting traditional stories to fit my format.

I am also indebted to Sherrill Fink for her skillful proofreading and for her excellent suggestions that improved the first manuscript. I take responsibility for errors that may appear in this final version.

I am especially thankful for my husband, Jay, for his encouragement, for his help with household chores, and for his taking care of the business end of publishing.

How to Use This Book

I believe we underestimate what young children are capable of learning. Our ideas are influenced by the school model, which aims most of its instruction at what it considers the largest population— the "average child." But when we teach to the average, we train our children to be…average! Instead, we can grow children who exceed the average by exposing them to above-average content—as long as that content is taught patiently, frequently, and consistently, and is reviewed often.

General Thoughts on Teaching Language

Learning rules without practical application is a sterile activity. Absorbing grammar incidentally without the guidance of rules is inefficient. By combining simple rules with continued "real life" use of those rules in language, the teacher lays the foundation for a child's application of appropriate rules to his own work in the future.

Children are natural imitators. This book provides you with examples of correctly spoken and written English in order to train the child's ear and hand. Then his original ideas can have form and beauty when they are expressed.

Every time a child speaks or writes correctly, that pattern is imprinted on his mind; the same is true for patterns that are incorrectly practiced. It is better to do less work, and do it correctly, than to practice errors. Then the child doesn't have to spend time unlearning and relearning.

So don't hurry through these lessons just to finish. Take the time to have the child answer in complete sentences. Take the time to frequently repeat rules until the child knows them. Take the time to have the child write correctly. Take the time to allow the child to make corrections immediately. If you require him to correct his mistakes, you will not damage his self-esteem. Compliment the correction and you will build his confidence.

Do not wait until a child is reading to expose him to good literature. Likewise, do not wait until a child is writing to expose him to proper use of our language. This is why I encourage the use of oral exercises while the child is young. Speech patterns are developed early. The longer a child uses incorrect language, the harder it will be to teach him correct speech and writing.

This early exposure is the purpose of my introducing young children to what some may consider advanced material. But this early introduction is not intended to result in mastery; mastery comes later.

I suggest you file the child's work in a notebook. This will serve as a way to organize all of his language work—narrations that you write for him, his copy work, his exercises, and copies of the letters he writes to real people.

The Method of This Book

First Language Lessons for the Well-Trained Mind combines the best of traditional content with examples and illustrations meaningful to present-day children. The scripted lessons focus on training the child in the proper use of standard English. They are not intended to be read by the child—instead, they aim to give you some idea of how to teach these skills. Appropriate answers that the child should give to your questions are suggested, but the child should certainly not be required to give those answers word for word! Do remember, though, to require all answers in complete sentences. If the child answers with a single word or phrase, reword the answer as a complete sentence, repeat it to the child, and ask him to repeat it back to you. This will begin to train his ear to recognize complete sentences.

This book covers grammar skills for grade 1. You will also need to provide a phonics/spelling program, formal penmanship instruction, and a writing program. *The Ordinary Parent's Guide to Teaching Reading* (phonics), published by Peace Hill Press, is designed to be completely compatible with *First Language Lessons.*

An elementary writing curriculum is also recommended. *First Language Lessons* covers grammar but does not cover beginning composition. The young writer should be encouraged to write across the curriculum, rather than doing isolated writing exercises related only to his grammar lessons. *Writing With Ease* by Susan Wise Bauer, also published by Peace Hill Press, is a step-by-step guide to developing elementary writing skills. The lessons are coordinated with *First Language Lessons* so that grammar concepts taught here are then reinforced by the *Writing With Ease* assignments.

Goals for Grade 1

1. To train the child's ear by allowing him to listen to correctly spoken language.
2. To train the child's speech by practicing correctly spoken grammar with him.
3. To train the child's attention by reading aloud to him and having him narrate back to you the content or story line, using proper grammar.
4. To teach beginning skills in grammar, capitalization, and punctuation.

Remember: exposure, not mastery, is the goal at this level!

The Tools Used in This Book: The "Four Strand" Approach

This book teaches rules and usage by using four different tools.

Strand 1: Memory work

The child is assigned simple memory work—short poems and brief rules and definitions to learn by heart. The poems instill the beauty and rhythm of correct language in the child's mind. The rules and definitions may not be completely understood when they are first committed to memory, but they will be a resource for the child as he[1] continues to exercise his growing language skills.

Strand 2: Copywork

Most first-grade students are not ready to do extensive written work. The first 41 lessons of this book are primarily oral. Beginning with Lesson 42, copywork exercises will appear where the grammar concept being taught requires written practice. These copywork exercises do not replace a writing program; they specifically target particular grammar skills. You should feel free to adapt the length of the assignment to the student's ability.

---

1   **A note on inclusive pronouns:** I studied advanced traditional grammar in the 1950s as part of my training in teacher certification. I learned that the pronouns "he" and "him" were generic pronouns, used to refer to both men and women. Although I understand why some users would prefer to see an alternate use of "he" and "she," I find this style of writing awkward; my early training shapes my usage! So I have used "he" and "him" to refer to the child throughout. If you prefer, simply change these pronouns to "she" and "her."

Strand 3: Narration

While the student is studying the basic principles of grammar, he is also learning how to produce original content orally. This will allow him to practice correct grammar at a time when he is still too young for extensive written work.

Two types of narration are used; both are intended to train the child in attention, observation, and expression, so that as he matures he will be able to share his own thoughts with eloquence.

a. Picture narration. Some of the lessons ask the student to look at and describe a picture. This allows him to practice observation skills as well as proper language use—always encourage the child to describe the picture in complete sentences!

b. Story narration. In other lessons, you will read a short story to the child and then ask him to tell you about it in his own words. This type of narration helps the child to listen with attention, to comprehend spoken language, and to grasp the main point of a work.

Strand 4: Grammar

The rules of grammar bring order to the chaos of words in the child's mind. Think of the study of formal grammar as the building of a room. The essentials—nouns and verbs—are the floor, walls, and ceiling. The room is decorated with adjectives and adverbs. The relationships between the different pieces of furniture in the room are demonstrated through prepositions and conjunctions. And sometimes the people in the room show intense emotion—with interjections!

The student is taught the correct definitions of grammatical terms from the very beginning. Lessons in oral usage are also provided so that the instructor can pinpoint any areas of difficulty in the child's use of language.

The lessons are planned to give an adequate foundation for every child. I assume that many children will not be ready to do a great deal of pencil-work in first grade. For children who are physically capable of doing more writing, I have provided "enrichment activities." But it is not necessary—or expected—that most children will do these enrichment exercises!

Plan on doing 2–3 lessons per week. Also plan on reviewing previous lessons as necessary, since the child may not remember material covered earlier. Young children forget more between the first-grade and second-grade years than in any other interval. Try to avoid a long break! Do not take three months off in the summer before continuing to the next level. Reviewing one lesson per week over the summer will prevent the child's forgetting the newly learned concepts.

Using the Lessons

Instructor: Suggested wording for the instructor is in traditional print.

Student: *Suggested wording for the student is in italics.*

Notes to Instructor *are indented, set in smaller type and in italics.*

Suggested wording that the student is to read or follow is in larger traditional print.

Definitions and terms are in larger bold print.

If you wish to gather all your materials for first grade in advance, you will need:
- a map of your state
- business-size envelopes and stamps
- a family calendar and a child's personal calendar
- scissors
- drawing supplies, crayons, highlighter markers
- a tape recorder
- colored construction paper
- old magazines to cut up
- a flower seed catalog

· · · · · · · · · · · · · · · · · ·   **LESSON 1**   · · · · · · · · · · · · · · · · · ·

Introducing common nouns

Instructor: Everything has a name. I will read the definition of a noun aloud to you three times.

Note to Instructor: *Repeat the following sentence three times.*

A noun is the name of a person, place, thing, or idea.

Instructor: We will talk about persons first. You are a person. Are you a boy or a girl?

Note to Instructor: *Encourage the student to answer in complete sentences. If he answers with a single word or fragment, turn his answer into a complete sentence and say it to him. Then ask him to repeat the sentence back to you.*

Student: *I am a _____.*

Instructor: "Boy" and "girl" are naming words that are common to a lot of persons, so we call them **common nouns**. Other naming words that are common to a lot of persons are words like "mother," "father," "sister," "brother," "grandmother," "grandfather," "aunt," "uncle," and "cousin."

Note to Instructor: *Repeat definition of a noun three more times, emphasizing the word <u>person</u>: "A noun is the name of a <u>person</u>, place, thing, or idea."*

• • • • • • • • • • • • • • • • • • • LESSON 2 • • • • • • • • • • • • • • • • • •

Introducing poem memorization: "The Caterpillar"

Notes to Instructor: *Read the poem to the student and discuss it before working on memorization. As a helpful technique to assist in memorization, try the following: On the first day that the poem is assigned, read the poem aloud to the student three times in a row. Repeat this triple reading twice more during the day, if possible. After the first day, read the poem aloud three times in a row once daily. (It may be more convenient to read the poem into a tape recorder three times, and then have the student replay the tape.) On the second day, and every day thereafter, ask the student to try to repeat parts of the poem along with you (or the tape recorder). When he can say the poem along with you, encourage him to repeat it first to a stuffed animal, then to himself in a mirror, and finally to "real people."*

Today, read "The Caterpillar" aloud three times in a row. Repeat twice more during the day. Don't forget to say the title and author as part of each repetition!

The Caterpillar[1]
Christina G. Rossetti

Brown and furry
Caterpillar in a hurry;
Take your walk
To the shady leaf, or stalk.

May no toad spy you,
May the little birds pass by you;
Spin and die,
To live again a butterfly.

---

1   Several versions of this poem have appeared in print. The best-known alternative version was first published by Macmillan in 1893 as part of *Sing-Song: A Nursery-Rhyme Book*:
Brown and furry
Caterpillar in a hurry,
Take your walk
To the shady leaf, or stalk,
Or what not,
Which may be the chosen spot.
No toad spy you,
Hovering bird of prey pass by you;
Spin and die,
To live again a butterfly.

LESSON 3

Common nouns (Family relationships)
Poem review: "The Caterpillar" (Lesson 2)

Note to Instructor: *Don't forget to review "The Caterpillar" today!*

Instructor: I will read the definition of a noun to you: **A noun is the name of a person, place, thing, or idea.**

Instructor: Try to say as much of it as you can with me, as I say this definition slowly three times more.

Together: **A noun is the name of a person, place, thing, or idea.**

Note to Instructor: *Repeat this definition three times along with the student.*

Instructor: The first part of the definition is "A noun is the name of a person…" You are a person. Are you a boy or a girl?

Student: *I am a_____.*

Instructor: "Boy" and "girl" are naming words that are common to a lot of persons, so we call them **common nouns.** The words "mother," "father," "sister," and "brother" are also common nouns. They name persons in families. Let's talk about persons in families. Families start with mothers and fathers. Everyone has a mother and a father. I will help you answer the following questions:

Note to Instructor: *Help the student answer each question in a complete sentence. Give the student plenty of help!*

Instructor: What do we call two girls who have the same mother and father?

Student: *Two girls who have the same mother and father are called sisters.*

Instructor: What do we call two boys who have the same mother and father?

Student: *Two boys who have the same mother and father are called brothers.*

Instructor: Sisters and brothers are persons who have the same mother and father! Do you know what your mother's mother is called?

Student: *My mother's mother is my grandmother.*

Instructor: What is your father's mother called?

Student: *My father's mother is my grandmother.*

Instructor: "Grandmother" is the common noun that names the mother of your mother or father! Do you know what your mother's father is called?

Student: *My mother's father is my grandfather.*

Instructor: What is your father's father called?

Student: *My father's father is my grandfather too.*

Instructor: "Grandfather" is the common noun that names the father of your mother or father! Remember: Mother, father, sister, brother, and grandfather are persons in families. Aunts, uncles, and cousins are also persons in families. An aunt is the sister of your mother or father. Do you have any aunts?

Student: *My aunt is Aunt _____.*

Instructor: An uncle is the brother of your mother or father. Do you have any uncles?

Student: *My uncle is Uncle _____.*

Instructor: "Uncle" and "aunt" are common nouns for the brother and sister of your mother and father! A cousin is the child of your aunt or uncle. Do you have any cousins?

Student: *My cousins are _____.*

Instructor: "Mother," "father," "sister," "brother," "grandfather," "aunt," "uncle," and "cousin" are all common nouns that name people.

·   **LESSON 4**   · · · · · · · · · · · · · · · · · ·

Proper nouns (First names)
Poem review: "The Caterpillar" (Lesson 2)

Notes to Instructor: *The instructor will need a pencil and paper for the lesson. The student will need a pencil and paper for the enrichment activity.*

Remember to review "The Caterpillar" today!

Remember that one of your goals is to teach the student to answer in complete sentences. Encourage the student to use the words of the question in his answer.

Instructor: I will read the definition of a noun to you. **A noun is the name of a person, place, thing, or idea.** Try to say as much of this definition of a noun as you can along with me. I will say it slowly three times more.

TOGETHER (three times): **A noun is the name of a person, place, thing, or idea.**

Instructor: The first part of the definition is: "A noun is the name of a person…" What is your name?
Student: *My name is_____ .*

Instructor: You are not just any boy or girl. You are _____ [use student's proper name]. This is your own special "proper" name. **Proper names** are the same as **proper nouns.** Proper nouns begin with a capital letter.

   Note to Instructor: *Write the student's name and show him the capital letter.*

Instructor: What is your mother's name?
Student: *My mother's name is _____.* [Either a proper name or "Mommy" is acceptable.]

Instructor: She is not just any mother—she is your special mother with a special name.

   Note to Instructor: *Print the special name of the student's mother. Point and show that the name begins with a capital letter.*

Instructor: Proper names begin with a capital letter. What is your father's name?
Student: *My father's name is_____.*

Instructor: He is not just any father, he is your special father with a special name.

   Note to Instructor: *Print the special name of the student's father. Point and show that the name begins with a capital letter.*

Instructor: Proper names begin with a capital letter. "Sister" and "brother" are naming words that are common to a lot of sisters and brothers in lots of families. Do you have a sister or brother? If you do, that sister or brother is one special person with a special name. What are the names of your sisters and brothers?

Note to Instructor: *If the student doesn't have sisters and brothers, you can substitute "friend" in the exercise below.*

Student: My sister's name is _____. My brother's name is_____.

Note to Instructor: *Print the name as the student gives it. Point to the first letter.*

Instructor: This is a capital letter. Proper names begin with a capital letter. These are the proper names of your brother and sister. These names tell you that they are not just any brother or sister. These names are special to them. These special, proper names begin with a capital letter.

Enrichment Activity

If the student is already writing easily, you may have him copy family names using correct capitalization.

····················· **LESSON 5** ·····················

Introducing story narration: "The Rabbit and the Turtle"

Notes to Instructor: *The instructor will need a pencil and paper.*

Narration is a skill to be learned through practice. In narration, the student simply tells back a story in his own words. There are two common difficulties in learning to narrate.

> *1. The student gives every detail of the story, making the narration too long to write down.*

> *2. The student doesn't know how to start or what to say.*

To help young students summarize, we have provided summary questions. After reading the story, ask the student the questions that follow. He should practice answering in complete sentences. If he answers with a phrase or single word, repeat his answer back to him as a complete sentence. Then ask him to repeat that sentence back to you. This begins to train the student to formulate grammatical sentences.

Then ask the student, "What is one thing you remember about the story?" Help him to phrase his answer as a complete sentence. You should then write the sentence down as he watches. Point out any capitalization or punctuation as you write.

If the student uses verbal "fillers" such as "uh," "like," or "you know," encourage him to stop and think in silence until he is ready to speak the sentence. When these "fillers" slip back into the narration, simply repeat what the student has said, omitting the useless word; then have him repeat after you.

There is no rush! This is a skill to be learned. You are training the student in thinking skills, so that he can grasp and retain more knowledge in his later stages of education. Narration exercises train the mind to grasp what is central—an essential skill for note-taking later on.

Read the following Aesop's Fable aloud to the student, and then ask the "starter questions" at the end of the story. Remember to encourage the student to answer in complete sentences. Then ask the student, "What is one thing you remember from the story?" Write his answer down and read it back to him.

The Rabbit and the Turtle

One day a rabbit made fun of a turtle. "How short your feet are! And how slowly you move!" he said. "Does it take you all day to walk to the table for breakfast?"

"My feet may be short," the turtle said, "but I can still beat you at a race!"

The rabbit laughed. He was sure that the little turtle could not possibly win! So he proposed that they run a race.

"All right," said the turtle, "but we need someone to declare the winner."

"Let's ask the fox," said the rabbit.

So they asked the fox to watch the race and decide on the winner. The fox said, "Ready, set, go!" And the race was on.

The turtle and the rabbit started out. The rabbit went leaping ahead in huge jumps and bounds. Soon he was far, far out of sight. The turtle plodded slowly along, so slowly that you could barely see him move.

The rabbit looked behind him. The turtle was nowhere in sight! And he was tired from all that leaping and bounding. So he decided to lie down beside the road and take a nap.

While he was sleeping, the turtle plodded right past him! When the rabbit woke up, he could just see, far in the distance, the turtle heading across the finish line.

He jumped up and ran as fast as he could. But before he could catch up, the turtle had crossed the line and won the race.

"The turtle is the winner!" the fox declared.

"Wait! Wait!" the rabbit cried. "I'm the faster runner!"

"That may be so," the fox said. "But the turtle has won this race. Remember: it is much better to be slow and steady than to be fast and lazy."

Moral: Slow and steady wins the race!

Note to Instructor: *Use these questions to help the student summarize the story.*

Instructor: What did the rabbit and turtle decide to do?
Student: *The rabbit and turtle decided to run a race.*

Instructor: Who watched the race for them?
Student: *The fox watched them.*

Instructor: Who was winning at first?
Student: *At first the rabbit was winning.*

Instructor: Then what did the rabbit do?
Student: *He decided to take a nap.*

Instructor: What did the turtle do while the rabbit was sleeping?
Student: *The turtle crossed the finish line while the rabbit was sleeping.*

Instructor: What is the moral of this story?
Student: *Slow and steady wins the race!*

· · · · · · · · · · · · · · · · · · · **LESSON 6** · · · · · · · · · · · · · · · · · ·

Proper nouns (First names)
Poem review: "The Caterpillar" (Lesson 2)

Note to Instructor: *The instructor will need a pencil and paper.*

Remember to review "The Caterpillar" today.

Instructor: Do you remember what a grandmother is?

Student: *My grandmother is my mother's mother or my father's mother.*

Instructor: Your grandmothers have special names. What are your two grandmothers' special names?

Student: *My grandmothers' special names are _____. [Either a given name or the grandmother's "family" name—Grammy, Maw-Maw, Granny, etc.—is acceptable.]*

Instructor: I will write those names down for you. Can you point to the capital letters that begin those names? These are the **proper names** of your grandmothers. Proper names are also called **proper nouns.**

Note to Instructor: *Write the names down and help the student point to the capital letters that begin them.*

Instructor: Do you remember what a grandfather is?

Student: *My grandfather is my mother's father or my father's father.*

Instructor: What are your grandfathers' special names?

Student: *My two grandfathers' special names are_____.*

Instructor: I will write those names down, too. These are the proper names of your grandfathers. Can you show me the capital letters that begin them?

Note to Instructor: *Write the names down and help the student find the capital letter at the beginning of each.*

········· **LESSON 7** ·················

Common and proper nouns

Instructor: Repeat the definition of a noun with me three times.

TOGETHER (three times): **A noun is the name of a person, place, thing, or idea.**

Instructor: We have talked about different kinds of people—mothers, fathers, sisters, brothers, grandmothers, grandfathers. All of these words are nouns, because they are the names of kinds of people. We call these **common nouns** because these words don't name a particular person. There are many mothers, fathers, sisters, brothers, grandmothers, and grandfathers in the world! Here are some other common nouns for kinds of people: "firefighter," "farmer," "teacher," "engineer," "doctor," and "nurse." Can you think of other common nouns for kinds of people?

Note to Instructor: *Help the student to think of other common nouns that name occupations.*

Instructor: Every firefighter, farmer, teacher, doctor, and nurse also has a special name. If the special name of the person is used, it is called a **proper noun**.

Note to Instructor: *Read the following pairs of sentences aloud to the student, pointing out common and proper nouns.*

The fire was put out by the firefighter.

Jonathan Mendel put out the fire.

Instructor: "Firefighter" is a common noun because it doesn't name any special firefighter. "Jonathan Mendel" is a proper noun because it names one special firefighter.

The doctor wore a white coat.

Susanna Wright wore a white coat.

Instructor: "Doctor" is a common noun because it doesn't name any special doctor. "Susanna Wright" is a proper noun because it names one special doctor.

·   **LESSON 8**   · · · · · · · · · · · · · · · · · · ·

Common and proper nouns
Poem review: "The Caterpillar" (Lesson 2)

Note to Instructor: *Remember to review "The Caterpillar" today.*

Instructor: Repeat the definition of a noun with me three times.

TOGETHER (three times): **A noun is the name of a person, place, thing, or idea.**

Instructor: Now can you say this definition all by yourself?
Student: *A noun is the name of a person, place, thing, or idea.*

Instructor: A noun is the name of a person, place, thing, or idea. A **common noun** is the name of a kind of person. A **proper noun** is a person's special, particular name. Let's talk some more about common and proper nouns.

Note to Instructor: *Read the following pairs of sentences aloud to the student, pointing out common and proper nouns.*

The teacher went to the store for some milk.

Maria Santilli went to the store for some milk.

Instructor: "Teacher" is a common noun because it doesn't name any special teacher. "Maria Santilli" is a proper noun because it names one special teacher.

The farmer grows corn.

Mark Elder grows corn.

Instructor: "Farmer" is a common noun because it doesn't name any special farmer. "Mark Elder" is a proper noun because it names one special farmer.

My mother ate cereal for breakfast.

_____ ate cereal for breakfast.

Note to Instructor: *Fill in the proper name of the student's mother.*

Instructor: "Mother" is a common noun because there are many, many mothers in the world. But
_____ is the special, proper name of your own mother. There is only one of those!

••••••••••••••••••••• **LESSON 9** •••••••••••••••••••••

Introducing picture narration: "Children Playing on the Beach"

Note to Instructor: *Like story narration, picture narration allows the young student to practice oral composition without forcing him to invent a topic. Picture narration also improves observation skills.*

Ask the following questions to help the student describe the picture. Remember to encourage the student to answer in complete sentences. If necessary, repeat fragmentary answers in the form of a complete sentence and then ask the student to repeat the complete sentence back to you. ("Where are the two little girls?" "On the beach." "Say that after me: The two little girls are on the beach.") Sample answers are provided, but any answer based on the picture is acceptable.

Instructor: Look at the picture while I tell you about the artist, Mary Cassatt. She was born in Pennsylvania in 1844—over a hundred and fifty years ago. When she was twenty-two, she went to Paris to study painting, but the art school she wanted to attend (the École des Beaux-Arts [ay KAWL day boh ZAHR]) wouldn't allow her in because she was a woman. Instead, she had to study privately with tutors.

Where are the two little girls?
Student: *The two little girls are on the beach.*

Instructor: The name of this painting is "Children Playing on the Beach." Are the two little girls dressed exactly the same?
Student: *No, one little girl is wearing a hat.*

Instructor: How many boats are on the water?
Student: *There are two boats on the water.*

Instructor: Are the two boats exactly the same?
Student: *No, one boat has sails.*

Instructor: What is the little girl without the hat doing?
Student: *She is filling her bucket with sand.*

Instructor: You can't really see what the other little girl is doing—but you can use your imagination. What do you think she might be doing?
Student: *The other little girl is [filling her bucket with sand OR digging a hole].*

Instructor: What kind of noun is "girl?" Is it a common noun or a proper noun?
Student: *It is a common noun.*

Instructor: The special, proper names of these two little girls are proper nouns, but we don't know what those names are. Use your imagination again. What do you think their proper names might be?

Student: *Their names are [Rachel] and [Mary].*

Note to Instructor: *You can view "Children Playing on the Beach" in the National Gallery of Art (www.nga. gov) collection online. Search for Mary Cassatt (do not use quotation marks around the name) or visit http:// www.nga.gov/collection/gallery/ggcassattptg/ggcassattptg-main1.html.*

·   **LESSON 10**   ·

Proper nouns (Writing the student's proper name)
Poem review: "The Caterpillar" (Lesson 2)

Note to Instructor: *Both the instructor and the student will need a pencil and paper.*

Review "The Caterpillar" today. Ask the student to say as much of it as he can alone. He should be able to repeat most or all of the poem from memory for you.

Instructor: I will read the definition of a noun aloud to you. Then, you say it with me when I say it again. **A noun is the name of a person, place, thing, or idea.** Now let's say that together.

TOGETHER: **A noun is the name of a person, place, thing, or idea.**

Instructor: Are you a person?
Student: *I am a person!*

Instructor: Are you just any person or are you one special person?
Student: *I am one special person.*

Instructor: What is your special name?
Student: *My name is _____.*

Note to Instructor: *The student can simply give his first name. Print the student's name. Point to the capital letter beginning his name.*

Instructor: This is your name. It is a special name, so it is called a proper noun. With what kind of letters do names begin?
Student: *Names begin with capital letters.*

Instructor: Let's say that together three times.

TOGETHER (three times): Names begin with capital letters.

Note to Instructor: *Have the student copy his first name today.*

Instructor: Your name is a special, proper noun because it names one special person—you!

••••••••••••••••••••••• LESSON 11 •••••••••••••••••••

Proper nouns (Writing first names)

Note to Instructor: *Both the instructor and the student will need a pencil and paper.*

Instructor: Let's review our definition of what a noun is. Repeat it with me two times:

TOGETHER (two times): **A noun is the name of a person, place, thing, or idea.**

Instructor: Now, can you repeat that definition alone?

Note to Instructor: *Prompt the student, if necessary.*

Instructor: Nouns that name many different persons are called common nouns. Are you a boy or a girl?

Student: *I am a _____ .*

Instructor: There are many boys and girls in the world, but what is your special name?

Student: *My name is _____ .*

Note to Instructor: *Remember to prompt the student to answer in complete sentences!*

Instructor: Your special name says that you are not just any boy or girl. We call your special name a **proper noun.** You have a mother and a father (and a sister and/or a brother and/or a friend). They all have proper names too! Let's write down the special names for all of these people.

Note to Instructor: *Print the proper names of each person in the student's family. Point out that each name begins with a capital letter. Then ask the student to copy his own first name twice, neatly. Remind him that it begins with a capital letter.*

Enrichment Activity

Ask the student to copy the first names of other family members.

· **LESSON 12** · · · · · · · · · · · · · · · · · · ·

Story narration: "The Lion and the Mouse"

Note to Instructor: *The instructor will need a pencil and paper.*

Read the following Aesop's Fable aloud to the student, and then ask the "starter questions" at the end of the story. Remember to encourage the student to answer in complete sentences. Then ask the student, "What is the one thing you remember from the story?" Write his answer down and read it back to him.

The Lion and the Mouse

One hot afternoon, a great lion lay sleeping in the shade. A little mouse, going back to his cool home underneath the roots of a nearby tree, accidentally ran across the lion's outstretched tail. The lion woke at once and grabbed the little creature with his huge paw.

"How dare you disturb my nap!" he growled. "I'll eat you for that!"

"Please, please don't eat me!" begged the little mouse. "Let me go, and I'll repay the favor one day—I'll help you when *you* need help!"

The lion laughed. "How could a tiny thing like you ever help a huge lion like me?" he chuckled. But he was so amused by the mouse's promise that he let the mouse go. The mouse skittered away to his little house, and the lion lay back down to finish his nap.

Several weeks later, the lion was hunting when he stepped into a great net, spread by hunters! The net closed over him at once. He struggled and struggled, but the strands only wrapped more tightly around him. Finally, he threw back his huge head and roared in distress.

From far away, the little mouse heard the lion's anguished roar. He ran as quickly as he could until he saw the lion's plight.

"Now it is my turn to help you!" the mouse exclaimed. He climbed up onto the lion's back and began to gnaw the thick ropes with his tiny teeth. One by one, the ropes gave way. Before long, the lion was free! He shook his mane with relief.

"Little mouse," he said, "I was wrong. I thought that you couldn't help me because you are so small. But you have saved my life. How glad I am that I spared you when you stepped on my tail!"

Moral: "Even a little one can help in times of trouble!"

Note to Instructor: *Use these questions to help the student summarize the story.*

Instructor: Which two animals were described in the fable?
Student: *The animals described in the fable were a lion and a mouse.*

Instructor: What did the mouse do that made the lion wake up?
Student: *The mouse ran across the lion's tail.*

Instructor: What did the lion think about doing?
Student: *The lion wanted to eat the mouse.*

Instructor: What did the mouse promise?
Student: *The mouse promised to help the lion if the lion would let him go.*

Instructor: Did the lion let the mouse go?
Student: *Yes, the lion let the mouse go.*

Instructor: How did the lion get into trouble?
Student: *He was trapped in a net by hunters.*

Instructor: How did the mouse set him free?
Student: *The mouse chewed the net apart with his teeth.*

Instructor: Was the lion grateful?
Student: *Yes, the lion thanked the mouse for helping him.*

•   **LESSON 13**   •

Proper nouns (Family names)
Poem review: "The Caterpillar" (Lesson 2)

Note to Instructor: *Both the instructor and the student will need a pencil and paper.*

Remember to review "The Caterpillar" today.

Instructor: I will read the definition of a noun to you: **A noun is the name of a person, place, thing, or idea.** Can you say that definition by yourself?

Note to Instructor: *Prompt the student, if necessary, to use the exact words of the definition.*

Instructor: First names are special names given to each person. Last names are names that you share with other members of your family. What is your first name?

Student: *My first name is _____.*

Instructor: What is your last name—your family name?

Student: *My last name is _____.*

Instructor: Family names are proper nouns, too. Your family is not just any family—it has its own special name! What are the first and last names of other members of your family?

Note to Instructor: *Talk with the student about various family members' first and last names. Then, let the student watch as you write his first and last name. Ask the student to copy his first and last name. Help him put his finger between the two names to space them properly.*

Enrichment Activity

Have the student copy the first and last names of other family members.

••••••••••••••••••••••• **LESSON 14** •••••••••••••••••••••

Proper nouns (Middle names)

Note to Instructor: *Both the instructor and the student will need a pencil and paper.*

Instructor: Say the definition of a noun with me three times: **A noun is the name of a person, place, thing, or idea.** We've talked about proper names—first and last names. What is your first name?

Student: *My first name is_____.*

Instructor: What is your last name—your family name?

Student: *My last name is _____.*

Instructor: Most people also have a middle name. A middle name is another, special name given to a child. What is your middle name?

Student: *My middle name is_____.*

Instructor: Let's write your middle name now.

Note to Instructor: *Write the student's middle name. Point out the capital letter. Have the student read his own middle name. Then add the student's first and last name on either side of the middle name.*

Instructor: What is your mother's middle name?

Note to Instructor: *Tell the student the answer, if necessary.*

Student: *My mother's middle name is _____.*

Instructor: What is your father's middle name?

Student: *My father's middle name is _____.*

Note to Instructor: *Write out the full names of the student's mother and father. Point out the first, middle, and last names. Then have the student copy his own full name. Show him how to space the words by putting his finger between each name.*

Enrichment Activity

Have the student copy the full names of family members.

• • • • • • • • • • • • • • • • • • LESSON 15 • • • • • • • • • • • • • • • •

Poem memorization: "Work"

Note to Instructor: *Read the poem aloud to the student three times now. Repeat this triple reading twice more during the day. Remember to read the title and author. Tell the student that "Anonymous" means we don't know who wrote the poem.*

Work

Anonymous

Work while you work,
Play while you play;
This is the way
To be happy each day.
All that you do,
Do with your might;
Things done by halves
Are never done right.

•••••••••••••••••••••   **LESSON 16**   ••••••••••••••••••••

Proper nouns (Full names)
Poem review: "Work" (Lesson 15)

Note to Instructor: *The instructor will need a pencil and paper.*

Have the student repeat the poem "Work" three times before beginning today's lesson.

Instructor: Can you say the definition of a noun for me?

Note to Instructor: *If necessary, prompt student to use the exact words: "A noun is the name of a person, place, thing, or idea."*

Instructor: First names and middle names are special names given to children. Last names are family names. All of these names are proper nouns. Let's talk about the first, middle, and last names of people in our family.

Note to Instructor: *Have the student tell you the full name of each family member. Supply names, if necessary! Don't forget grandparents; include aunts, uncles, and cousins if you wish. Write each name as the student says it. Point out the capital letters.*

Instructor: Now practice writing your own full name.

Note to Instructor: *Write the student's full name. Have the student copy it, again showing him how to space the words by putting his finger between each name.*

Enrichment Activity

Have the student write his own name from memory.

• LESSON 17 •

Common nouns (Names of places)
Poem review: "Work" (Lesson 15)

Note to Instructor: *Remember to review "Work" today!*

Instructor: Say the definition of a noun with me.

Together: **A noun is the name of a person, place, thing, or idea.**

Instructor: We have learned about names of people. Now let's learn about names of places. What room are we in?

Student: *We are in the _____. [kitchen, living room, etc.]*

Instructor: This room is a place. This room is in a house (or apartment). This house (or apartment) is also a place. And this house (or apartment) is in a city (or town, or county). Words like "kitchen," "bedroom," "house," "apartment," "city," "town," and "county" are nouns because they name places. All of these names are **common nouns**. There are lots of kitchens, bedrooms, houses, cities, and towns! We call all of these words common nouns because they could be naming any kitchen, bedroom, house, city, or town. Other words that name common kinds of places are words like "mountain," "hill," "yard," "street," "road," "sidewalk," "museum…" Let's name some other places together.

Note to Instructor: *Prompt the student to think of other names of places. Look out the window, use pictures, or walk around the house or yard. Remember to prompt the student for common nouns that name places.*

Instructor: All of these names tell us about places. They are all common nouns. Remember: A noun is the name of a person or place.

• • • • • • • • • • • • • • • • • • •   **LESSON 18**   • • • • • • • • • • • • • • • • • • •

Proper nouns (Places: your city and state)
Poem review: "The Caterpillar" (Lesson 2) and
"Work" (Lesson 15)

Note to Instructor: *The instructor will need a pencil and paper.*

Today, review both "The Caterpillar" and "Work." Don't be surprised if the student has forgotten some of "The Caterpillar." Allow him to read it or listen to you recite it in order to refresh his memory.

Instructor: Say the definition of a noun three times with me.

Together (three times): **A noun is the name of a person, place, thing, or idea.**

Instructor: What room are you in?
Student: *I am in the _____.*

Instructor: This room is in a house (or apartment). This house (apartment) is in a city (town, county). Do you know the name of this city (town, county)?
Student: *This city (town, county) is _____. [Tell student the name, if necessary.]*

Instructor: (Name of city, town, or county) is not just any place. It is one special place where you live! This name is the special, proper name of your city (town, county). We call names like this **proper nouns**. I will write the proper name of the place where you live.

Note to Instructor: *Write the proper name of the place where your student lives. Show him that it begins with a capital letter.*

Instructor: Your city (town, county) is in a special state. That state is _____. It is not just any state—it is one special state, with its own name. This special name is also a proper noun. When you write the name of your city (town, county), you write the name of the state next to it.

Note to Instructor: *Write out the name of the state next to the city (town, county). Put a comma between the two names (Chicago, Illinois; Austin, Texas; Louisa County, Virginia). Point out the capital letters. Ask the student to repeat the place name and state together three times.*

Enrichment Activity

Have the student copy the proper name of the place where he lives. Remind him to put a comma between the town and the state.

··········· **LESSON 19** ···············

Proper nouns (Places)
Poem review: "Work" (Lesson 15)

Note to Instructor: *Be sure to review "Work" today!*

You will need a map of your state for today's lesson.

The student will need a pencil and paper for the enrichment activity.

Instructor: Say the definition of a noun for me.

Student: **A noun is the name of a person, place, thing, or idea.**

Instructor: We have been talking about names of places—common names, like "town," "city," "county," "state," "bedroom," "kitchen," and proper names, like _____ (use name of student's city, town, or county). We also talked about the proper name of your state. Do you remember your city (town, county) and state?

Student: *I live in _____. [Prompt student to use "I live in"; also remind him of the proper names of his city and state, if necessary.]*

Instructor: (City and state) are **proper nouns**. They are the special names of the city (town, county) and state where you live. There are many other places in your state. There are mountains, rivers, parks, hills, streets, roads, valleys, cities, and towns. All of these nouns name places. They are all common nouns. But most of these places also have special names—proper names. Let's look on a map of our state and find some of these proper names.

Note to Instructor: *Look at a map of your state together. Help the student identify mountains, rivers, and other geographical features. Read together the proper name of each place. Remind the student that each proper name is a noun. Point out the capital letters at the beginning of each proper name. Explain to the student that to make things clear in a crowded place, maps often print important names in all capital letters.*

Enrichment Activity

Ask the student to practice writing the name of his city and state from memory, placing a comma between the city and state.

·   **LESSON 20**   ·

Proper nouns (States)

Note to Instructor: *Have the student copy his name before beginning today's lesson.*

The student will need a pencil and paper for the enrichment activity.

Instructor: Do you remember the proper name of the state in which you live?

Student: *I live in _____.*

Instructor: That is only one state, but there are fifty states in the United States. "State" is a common noun—it could refer to any of those states. But each state has its own special name. Those names are **proper nouns**. Let's look at some of the state names together.

Note to Instructor: *Point to the different state names on the following page and practice saying them. Remind the student that each one begins with a capital letter. Explain to the student that to make things clear in a crowded space, maps often print important names in all capital letters. Be sure to identify states where different family members and friends may live or where the student has visited for vacations. Print some states with only the first letter capitalized for the student to see.*

Enrichment Activity

The student may practice writing names of the states where friends and family live. Remind the student that these are proper names and should begin with capital letters.

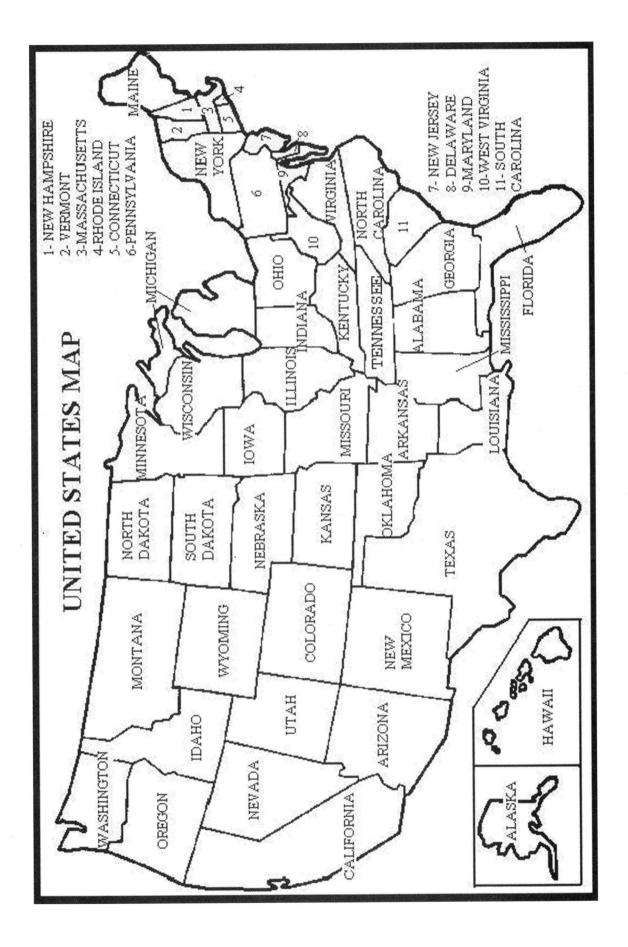

UNITED STATES MAP

1- NEW HAMPSHIRE
2- VERMONT
3-MASSACHUSETTS
4-RHODE ISLAND
5- CONNECTICUT
6-PENNSYLVANIA

7- NEW JERSEY
8- DELAWARE
9-MARYLAND
10-WEST VIRGINIA
11- SOUTH CAROLINA

WASHINGTON
OREGON
MONTANA
IDAHO
WYOMING
NEVADA
UTAH
CALIFORNIA
ARIZONA
COLORADO
NEW MEXICO
NORTH DAKOTA
SOUTH DAKOTA
NEBRASKA
KANSAS
OKLAHOMA
TEXAS
MINNESOTA
IOWA
MISSOURI
ARKANSAS
LOUISIANA
WISCONSIN
MICHIGAN
ILLINOIS
INDIANA
OHIO
KENTUCKY
TENNESSEE
MISSISSIPPI
ALABAMA
GEORGIA
FLORIDA
NEW YORK
MAINE
VIRGINIA
NORTH CAROLINA

HAWAII
ALASKA

••••••••••••••••••••• **LESSON 21** •••••••••••••••••••••

Proper nouns (Your address)
Poem review: "The Caterpillar" (Lesson 2) and
"Work" (Lesson 15)

Note to Instructor: *The instructor will need a pencil and paper for the lesson. The student will need a pencil and paper for the enrichment activity.*

Be sure to review "The Caterpillar" and "Work" today!

Instructor: Do you remember the name of your city and state? (Prompt the student, if necessary. Ask the student to repeat the city-state combination several times.) You live on _____. (Provide name of the student's street or road.) That is your street's special name. It is a **proper noun**, so we write it with a capital letter. I will write it down for you.

Note to Instructor: *Write the name of the student's street. Point out the capital letter.*

Instructor: You aren't the only person who lives on this street. Your house has a special number that goes with it. This number doesn't belong to any other house on the street! The number of your house, along with the street name, is your street address. When we write down your street address, your city, and your state, we have written your full address.

Note to Instructor: *Let the student watch you write out his entire address except the ZIP code (do not abbreviate state). ZIP codes will be done later. Both of you read the address, pointing to each capital letter. As you write, point to each capital letter.*

Instructor: Addresses are names of special places, so we call them proper nouns. Proper nouns begin with capital letters.

Note to Instructor: *Have the student repeat his address three times.*

Enrichment Activity

The student may write from memory the name of his city and state, placing a comma between the city and state. The student may also copy his own address.

Story narration: "The Little Girl Who Wanted to Be Dirty"

Note to Instructor: *The instructor will need a pencil and paper.*

Read the following old tale aloud to the student, and then ask the "starter questions" at the end of the story. Remember to encourage the student to answer in complete sentences. Then ask the student, "What is the one thing you remember from the story?" Write his answer down and read it back to him.

The Little Girl Who Wanted to Be Dirty

There once was a little girl who cried and screamed every time her mother wanted to give her a bath. "I like being dirty, and I hate to take baths!" was the little girl's reply each time her mother made her bathe. Her mother told her often, "If you don't bathe, you will be as dirty as a pig!" But the little girl wanted to be dirty—and she thought that she would love to be as dirty as a pig.

One night the little girl lay thinking about pigs. "I wish I were living in a pig pen," she thought. "I could wallow and play in soft cool mud all day. And at night I could just snuggle right down in the mud and sleep. I would never have to wash again!"

Suddenly she looked around. She wasn't in her clean white bed anymore. She was lying in the middle of a pigpen! The sun was shining down on her. It was warm and beautiful outside. She sat up. Mud dripped down the back of her neck. It felt wonderful! Mud squished between her fingers and her toes. There were three cute little pigs in the pen. They ran up to her and pushed at her with their noses. They wanted to play!

She jumped up and played tag with the pigs. They splattered mud all over each other! Then they played pig-in-the-middle and stuck-in-the-mud. When they were tired of playing, they all piled up into a big muddy heap for a rest.

Soon the little girl heard a voice calling, "Supper!" She was hungry from all that play. She jumped up and ran to the pig trough. But all she found there was slop! Old corncobs, bits of leftover sandwiches, tops of tomatoes, broken half-eaten cookies, and rotten potatoes. Her pig friends were eating happily. But the little girl began to cry. This wasn't her idea of a good supper! The sun was going down, and her fingers and toes were wet and cold. Mud had dried in her hair, and it made her head itch. Mud was smeared all down her face and neck. Her clothes were stiff with mud.

"I want to go home!" she said. So she crept out of the pigpen, down the road, until she got to her own house. She sneaked in the back door of her house, up the stairs and into the bathroom. Then she ran a tub of clean warm water with bubbles. She scrubbed off all of the dirt, put on fresh flowered pajamas, and sank into her soft bed, snuggling her head on her favorite pillow.

When she awoke the next morning, she ran to her mother to tell her all about it. "You have had a dream," said Mother.

"Oh, Mother," said the little girl, "it was a good dream because it made me want to be clean!"

Note to Instructor: *Use these questions to help the student summarize the story.*

Instructor: Did the little girl know that she was having a dream?
Student: *No, the little girl thought she was really in a pigpen.*

Instructor: Did she like the pigpen at first?
Student: *Yes, the little girl liked the pigpen.*

Instructor: Why did she like it?
Student: *The little girl got to squish in the mud and to play with the pigs.*

Instructor: What did she get for supper?
Student: *The little girl got old rotten food, like the pigs.*

Instructor: Did she still like the mud?
Student: *No, the little girl wanted to be clean.*

Instructor: How did the little girl get clean?
Student: *She went home and took a bath.*

Instructor: Did the dream change the way she thought about baths?
Student: *Yes, the dream made the little girl want to have a bath.*

•••••••••••••••••••••   **LESSON 23**   ••••••••••••••••••

Common nouns (Things)

Note to Instructor: *The student will need a pencil and paper.*

Ask the student to practice writing his name before beginning today's lesson.

Instructor: Let's say the definition of a noun together.

TOGETHER: **A noun is the name of a person, place, thing, or idea.**

Instructor: We have talked about names of people—common names like "boy," "girl," "mother," "father," "firefighter" and "teacher." These names are **common nouns**. We have also talked about proper names—the special names that each person has. These are **proper nouns**. We've also talked about names of places. These are nouns, too. Do you remember some common nouns that are places? (Prompt the student: kitchen, bedroom, town, city, river, mountain, etc.) Most places also have a special name—a proper noun. Do you remember any of the special names for these places? (Prompt the student with the proper names of places you have discussed.) Now we will talk about the third kind of noun: things. Nouns are also the names of things.

Note to Instructor: *Ask the student to name things he can see in the house and outside. Ask him to name things he uses for school, things he eats, and things he wears.*

Instructor: All of these names are common nouns. They are nouns because they are names of things. They are common nouns because you can find these things in many different places. Remember: **A noun is the name of a person, place, thing, or idea.** Now can you recite the definition of a noun for me?

Student: *A noun is the name of a person, place, thing, or idea.*

Note to Instructor: *Help, if necessary, by saying the definition with the student and by ending with a sincere compliment.*

·   **LESSON 24**   · · · · · · · · · · · · · · · · · ·

Picture narration: "The Family"

Note to Instructor: *The student will need a pencil and paper.*

Begin the lesson by asking the student to write (or copy) his full name.

Instructor:	This is another painting by the American artist Mary Cassatt. We've already looked at one picture by Mary Cassatt. Do you remember what the two children in that picture were doing?
Student:	*They were playing on the beach.*

Instructor:	Look carefully at this picture. How many children are in this picture?
Student:	*There are two children in the picture.*

Instructor:	Who is with them?
Student:	*Their mother is with them.*

Instructor:	What is the little girl holding?
Student:	*She is holding a flower.*

Instructor:	What is the baby looking at?
Student:	*The baby is looking at the little girl OR the flower.*

Instructor:	This painting is called "The Family." "Family" is a common noun. This family also has a proper name—a family name. Use your imagination and tell me what you think their family name might be?
Student:	*Their family name might be [name].*

Note to Instructor: *If the student cannot think of a family name, you can list the following and ask him to choose one: Clark, Snyder, Taylor, Perry, Martinez, Reddy, Singer, Gordon.*

Instructor:	Let's imagine what the little girl's full, proper name might be. What do you think her first name might be?
Student:	*Her name might be [Julia].*

Instructor:	What do you think her middle name might be?
Student:	*Her middle name might be [Marie].*

Instructor:	Let's imagine that her full name is [Julia Marie Snyder]. Do you think that the baby is her little brother or her little sister?

Student: *The baby is her little [brother OR sister].*

Instructor: What do you think the baby is about to do?
Student: *The baby is about to [climb off the mother's lap OR grab the flower].*

Instructor: Tell me one more thing that you see in the painting.
Student: *I see [trees OR a path OR grass].*

Note to Instructor: *You can view "The Family" in the Chrysler Museum (www.chrysler.org) collection online. Search for "Mary Cassatt" or visit http://www.chrysler.org/american01.asp.*

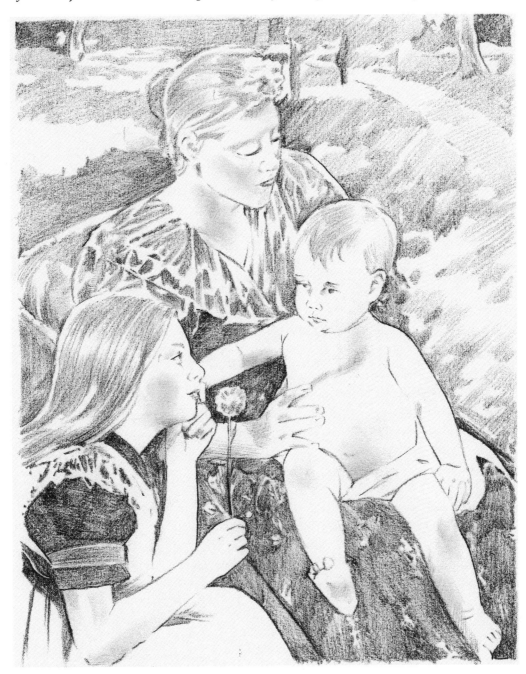

••••••••••••••••••••• **LESSON 25** •••••••••••••••••••••

Proper nouns (Aunts and uncles)
Introducing oral usage: "Avoiding 'ain't'"
Poem review: "The Caterpillar" (Lesson 2) and
"Work" (Lesson 15)

Notes to Instructor: *The instructor will need a pencil and paper for the lesson. The student will need a pencil and paper for the enrichment activity.*

Review "The Caterpillar" and "Work" today.

Lessons 25–26 are about the family relationship of uncles, aunts, and cousins. You should feel free to omit any part of these lessons if the student does not have uncles, aunts, or cousins to talk about.

Instructor: Say the definition of a noun with me three times.

Together (three times): **A noun is the name of a person, place, thing, or idea.**

Instructor: The words "aunt" and "uncle" name kinds of persons. What are aunts?
Student: *My aunt is my mother's [or father's] sister.*

Instructor: Do you have an aunt? (Does your mother or father have a sister?) What is your aunt's name?
Student: *My aunt's name is _____.*

Note to Instructor: *If your student has more than one aunt, repeat the exercise until all aunts are named. After you have done this oral work, you should write out the answers in sentences and show this to the student ("My aunt's name is_____.") Remind the student that this is not just any aunt, but names one special aunt, and so the aunt's name begins with a capital letter.*

Instructor: What are uncles?
Student: *Uncles are brothers of my mother or father.*

Instructor: Do you have an uncle? What is your uncle's name?
Student: My uncle's name is_____. (Example: Don) My other uncles are_____.

Note to Instructor: *Write for the student, "My uncle's name is ____." Show the student that this is not just any uncle, but one special uncle, and so the uncle's name begins with a capital letter.*

Oral Usage Exercise

Note to Instructor: *Beginning with this lesson, oral practice in correct usage will be included in some lessons. The rules cited in the "Note to Instructor" are for the instructor's information. They are not to be "taught" to a young student. Rather, the student's ear should be trained to recognize correct usage.*

Most usage problems occur with state-of-being verbs (am, is, are, was, were, be, being, been) and helping verbs (have, has, had, do, does, did, shall, will, should, would, may, might, must, can, could). At this level we will be practicing only correct usage; we are not yet ready to define "state of being" and "helping." This first oral usage practice avoids the use of "ain't," which is now used only in dialect or illiterate speech. Standard English uses "am not," "are not," "is not," "has not," or "have not." If the student uses an incorrect form, give him the correct form and ask him to repeat it.

Instructor: I will ask you a question. I want you to answer the question starting with the word "No." Isn't Aunt Lucy coming today?

Student: *No, she isn't coming today.*

Instructor: Isn't Uncle Hector coming tomorrow?

Student: *No, he isn't coming tomorrow.*

Instructor: Isn't your cousin Davis coming this summer?

Student: *No, he isn't coming this summer.*

· · · · · · · · · · · · · · · LESSON 26 · · · · · · · · · · · · · · ·

Proper nouns (Cousins)
Poem review: "The Caterpillar" (Lesson 2) and
"Work" (Lesson 15)

Note to Instructor: *The instructor will need a pencil and paper for the lesson. The student will need a pencil and paper for the enrichment activity.*

Review "The Caterpillar" and "Work" today.

Instructor: Last lesson we talked about uncles and aunts. Do you remember whom we talked about? Today we are going to talk about the children of those aunts and uncles. Children of your aunts and uncles are called your cousins. The word "cousin" doesn't name any particular person, so the word "cousin" is a common name for lots of people. But if we name the name of a particular, special cousin, that name is a proper noun. Do you have any cousins? What are their names?

Note to Instructor: *As the student gives the names of real cousins, write down their first, middle, and last names in a complete sentence. If the student can read, have him read it aloud to you.*

Student: [_____ _____ _____] is my cousin.

Note to Instructor: *Point out to the student which are first, middle, and last names. If they were named for other family members, tell the student about that. Do this exercise for two or three cousins—more if there is time and interest.*

Instructor: Who are cousins?
Student: *Cousins are children of my aunts and uncles.*

Enrichment Activity

Ask the student to write the names of his cousins. Then have the student copy or write sentences showing relationships, for example, "My cousin Mary Jane is Aunt Joan's daughter."

••••••••••••••••••••••• **LESSON 27** •••••••••••••••••••••

Poem memorization: "Hearts Are Like Doors"

Note to Instructor: *Read this new poem aloud to the student three times in a row now, and three more times at some point later in the day.*

Hearts Are Like Doors
Anonymous

Hearts, like doors, will open with ease,
To very, very little keys,
And don't forget that two of these
Are "Thank you, sir" and "If you please!"

······················ **LESSON 28** ·······················

Common and proper nouns (Family relationships and places)

Note to Instructor: *The instructor will need a pencil and paper.*

Read the poem "Hearts Are Like Doors" (Lesson 27) out loud to the student three times in a row.

Instructor: Say with me the definition of a noun.

TOGETHER: **A noun is the name of a person, place, thing, or idea.**

Instructor: Remember that special proper names of persons and places begin with a capital letter. Your address and the addresses of where other people live are special proper names of those places, so they are written with capital letters. I am going to write your address and the address of (choose another person the student knows). These are special, particular places—proper nouns—and so we write them with capital letters.

Note to Instructor: *Write the addresses as the student watches. Point out the capital letters in the special "proper" names.*

Instructor: Remember how we talked about common names of people like "mother," "father," "sister," "brother," "grandmother," "grandfather," "aunt," "uncle," "cousin." These words could mean people in anyone's family. Let's name the special proper names of these people in our family.

Note to Instructor: *Let the student watch you write the "proper name" as you say the sentences. Example: "My mother's name is _____. My father's name is _____."*

Enrichment Activity

The student may copy the full name of his mother or father (or other family names).

· **LESSON 29** ·

Proper nouns (Your address and ZIP code)
Poem review: "Hearts Are Like Doors" (Lesson 27)

Note to Instructor: *The instructor will need a pencil and paper for the lesson as well as an envelope for the enrichment activity.*

Have the student repeat the poem "Hearts Are Like Doors" three times in a row today.

Instructor: Last lesson we talked about common names of people like "mother" and "father." Then I showed you the special, proper names of those people. Today we are going to talk about "sister" and "brother." These words could mean people in anyone's family. Let's name the special proper names, also called **proper nouns**, of these people in our family.

Note to Instructor: *Let the student watch you write the "proper name" as you say the sentences. (Example: My sister's name is_____. My brother's name is_____.)*

Instructor: Now let's talk about something a little different. We already learned your address. But there's one more part of it you need to know. In an address, a ZIP code is a number after the state that tells the post office what part of the country you live in. Your ZIP code is_____.

Note to Instructor: *Write your ZIP code and read it to the student. Practice having him say it with you.*

Instructor: What is the name of the street (or road) on which you live?
Student: I live on _____.

Note to Instructor: *Have the student watch as you write his address. Write the number of his street or road, the name of his street or road, and on the next line, write his town, state (full spelling), and ZIP code. Abbreviations will be studied later.*

Instructor: This is your address. All the words in an address begin with capital letters. They are proper nouns because they name a special, particular place.

Note to Instructor: *Read the address with the student, pointing to the capital letters as you say the following reminder:*

Instructor: Names of streets, roads, cities, towns, counties, and states begin with capital letters. They are special, particular places. Say with me the definition of a noun.

Together: **A noun is the name of a person, place, thing, or idea.**

Instructor: Can you say that alone?

Note to Instructor: *Have the student repeat the definition of a noun to you.*

Enrichment Activity

Let the student watch you address a real envelope with the student's name and complete address, including ZIP code. Have the student draw a picture or write a message to be mailed back to him. Mail the letter!

•   **LESSON 30**   • • • • • • • • • • • • • • • • • • •

Common and proper nouns

Note to Instructor: *The instructor will need a pencil and paper for the lesson as well as drawing supplies for the enrichment activity.*

Instructor: Say with me the definition of a noun.

TOGETHER: **A noun is the name of a person, place, thing, or idea.**

Instructor: Look around the room and name common things you see that don't have special names.

Note to Instructor: *Prompt student, if necessary—curtain, paper, rug, window, or table.*

Instructor: We have already talked about common names of people like "mother," "father," "sister," "brother," "grandmother," and "grandfather." These words could mean people in anyone's family. But these people also have proper names. Today we are going to name the special proper names of your grandmother and grandfather.

Note to Instructor: *Let the student watch you write the proper name as you say the sentences. (Example: My grandmother's name is _____. My grandfather's name is _____.)*

Enrichment Activity

Draw a picture of things in a room. Label the things. Title the picture "Common Nouns."

············· **LESSON 31** ··················

Common nouns (Living things)
Oral usage: "Was/Were"
Poem review: "Hearts Are Like Doors" (Lesson 27)

Note to Instructor: *Don't forget to review the poem "Hearts Are Like Doors" today.*

Instructor: Let's say the definition of a noun together.

TOGETHER: **A noun is the name of a person, place, thing, or idea**.

Instructor: We have talked about names of people, places, and things. Did you know that names of animals are nouns, too? The names of all living things are nouns. Insects are living things. Can you name some insects for me?

Student: *Flies, mosquitoes, bees are insects.*

Instructor: Fish and sea life are living things. Name some things that live in the water.

Student: *Crabs, goldfish, water lilies, sharks live in the water.*

Instructor: Plants are living things. Name some trees.

Student: *Maple, oak, pine are trees.*

Instructor: Name some vegetables.

Student: *Tomatoes, potatoes, lettuce are vegetables.*

Instructor: Name some fruit.

Student: *Apples, oranges, grapes are fruit.*

Instructor: Name some nuts.

Student: *Pecans, walnuts are nuts.*

Instructor: Flowers are living things. Name some flowers.

Student: *Tulips, roses are flowers.*

Instructor: Animals are living things! Name some animals.

Student: *Cats, hamsters, dogs are animals.*

Instructor: All of the words we talked about today are nouns because they tell what the living things are named.

Oral Usage Exercise

Note to Instructor: *Use "was" and "were" to tell about something that happened in the past. Use "was" to tell about one person or thing. Use "were" to tell about more than one person or thing. Always use "were" with the word "you."*

Instructor: I will ask you a question. I want you to answer the question starting with the word "Yes."

Instructor: Was the kitten too little to walk?
Student: *Yes, the kitten was too little to walk.*

Instructor: Were the kittens grey and black?
Student: *Yes, the kittens were grey and black.*

Instructor: Were you cuddling the kittens?
Student: *Yes, I was cuddling the kittens.*

Instructor: Was I feeding the kittens?
Student: *Yes, you were feeding the kittens.*

························ **LESSON 32** ························

Common and proper nouns
(Family relationships and living things)

Note to Instructor: *The instructor will need a pencil and paper for the lesson. The student will need a pencil and paper for the enrichment activity.*

Instructor: Names of animals are **common nouns**. But some animals have special proper names, too! If you give a pet a special proper name, that name would be written with a capital letter. I am going to write some sentences for you to look at. They show the difference between common and **proper nouns** as names of pets.

Note to Instructor: *Write sentences that include the common and proper names of pets ("My cat's name is Fluffy," or "Lily's mouse is named Chang"). If the student has a pet, or knows the name of someone else's pet, use those real names for this exercise.*

Instructor: Remember how we talked about common names of people like "mother," "father," "sister," "brother," "grandmother," and "grandfather," "aunts," "uncles," and "cousins?" These words could mean people in anyone's family. Today we are going to name the special proper names of these people in our family.

Note to Instructor: *Choose any members of your family. Help the student to give the family member's proper name ("My aunt's name is_____"—either "Aunt Sabrina" or "Sabrina Cortez" is correct). Write out the sentence as you say it. Let the student watch you write. Point out that you are beginning proper names with capital letters.*

Enrichment Activity

If the student has a pet, ask him to write the common and proper name of the pet.

•••••••••••••••••••• **LESSON 33** ••••••••••••••••••••

Picture narration: "Master Bedroom"

Instructor: Look carefully at the picture while I tell you about the artist, Andrew Wyeth. Just like Mary Cassatt, Andrew Wyeth was born in Pennsylvania, but he was born in 1917—about seventy-five years after Mary Cassatt. He just died recently, in the year 2009. Andrew's father was also an artist. His name was N. C. Wyeth, and he illustrated many famous books, including books about Robin Hood and King Arthur. Andrew Wyeth used a kind of paint called "tempera" in most of his paintings. Tempera paint was made by adding colors to egg yolk.

What kind of room is in the painting?

Student: *It is a bedroom.*

Instructor: This painting is called "Master Bedroom." The master bedroom is the main bedroom in a house. Right now, the owner of the house isn't sleeping on the bed. Who is sleeping on the bed?

Student: *A dog is sleeping on the bed.*

Instructor: You've learned that a noun is a person, place, thing, or idea. The master bedroom is a place. The dog is a living thing. Can you name three other things that you can see in this painting?

Student: *I can see [a bed, a bedspread, a tree, a wall, a window].*

Instructor: Is "dog" a common noun or a proper noun?

Student: *Dog is a common noun.*

Instructor: What do you think the proper, special name of the dog is? Use your imagination.

Student: *His name is [Max].*

Instructor: [Max] looks like he's had a busy day! What do you think he's been doing?

Student: *He's been [chasing rabbits OR on a long walk with his master].*

Instructor: What two things can you see out of the bedroom window?

Student: *I can see a tree and a building.*

Instructor: When [Max's] master comes home, what do you think he will do?

Student: *He will [chase Max off the bed OR feed Max].*

Note to Instructor: *"Master Bedroom" is in a private collection. You can view color prints of the painting "Master Bedroom" at online print galleries such as artinthepicture.com, allposters.com, and andrew-wyeth-prints.com. Search for "Master Bedroom."*

••••••••••••••••••••• **LESSON 34** •••••••••••••••••••••

Proper nouns (Days of the week)
Poem review: "The Caterpillar" (Lesson 2),
"Work" (Lesson 15), and
"Hearts Are Like Doors" (Lesson 27)

Note to Instructor: *The instructor will need a calendar for the lesson as well as pencil, paper, and scissors for the enrichment activity.*

Don't forget to review "The Caterpillar," "Work," and "Hearts Are Like Doors" today.

Instructor: Remember our definition of a noun? Say it with me.

Together: **A noun is the name or a person, place, thing, or idea**.

Instructor: Today we are going to name the days of the week.

Note to Instructor: *Use a real calendar and point to the days. Some calendars begin with Sunday as the first day of the week; others begin with Monday. Use a calendar that shows the day your family considers to be the first day of the week.*

Instructor: There are seven days in a week—Sunday, Monday, Tuesday, Wednesday, Thursday, Friday, and Saturday. These are not just any days. Each day of the week has its own special proper name. It begins with a capital letter.

Note to Instructor: *On your calendar, show the student the capital letters at the beginning of each day of the week. If your calendar has the days in all capitals or abbreviations, write the days of the week for the student, showing him that each name starts with a capital letter. Say the names of the days of the week aloud with the student three times, pointing to each name as you say it. Help the student to find today's day on the calendar.*

Enrichment Activity

On a sheet of lined paper, write the days of the week in a column, skipping lines. Have the student cut them apart, mix them up, and then rearrange them in order. (If you save these names in an envelope, you can do this activity as often as needed, without having to rewrite them.)

•   **LESSON 35**   •

Poem memorization: "Days of the Week"
Common and proper nouns
Poem review: "Hearts Are Like Doors" (Lesson 27)

Note to Instructor: *The instructor will need a pencil and paper.*

Review "Hearts Are Like Doors" today. Then read "Days of the Week" aloud to the student three times in a row. Repeat this triple reading twice more during the day.

Days of the Week
Mother Goose rhyme, adapted by Sara Buffington

> Monday's child is fair of face,
>
> Tuesday's child is full of grace;
>
> Wednesday's child is ever so sweet,
>
> Thursday's child is tidy and neat;
>
> Friday's child is prone to a giggle,
>
> Saturday's child is easy to tickle;
>
> But the child that is born on restful Sunday
>
> Is happy and cheerful, and loves to play.

Instructor: Today we are going to review common and proper nouns. Common nouns for persons are: "girl," "boy," "man." Let's give a special proper name for each of these words.

Note to Instructor: *Help the student select real people he knows. Write the common noun and the proper noun for each, as in the example that follows: girl – Maria, boy – Jamal, man – Mr. Baxter.*

Instructor: Common nouns for places are: "store," "library," "zoo," "park." Let's give a special proper name for each of these places.

Note to Instructor: *Write the common and proper nouns for each place, as in the example that follows:*

store – (Name a store in which your student sees you shop.)

library – (Name the library you visit.)

zoo or park – (Name a zoo or park you have visited.)

Instructor: Other common nouns for things are: "cereal," "cookies," "toys," and "books." Let's give a special proper noun for each of these things.

Note to Instructor: *Write the common and proper nouns for each thing, as in the example that follows:*

cereal – Cheerios

cookies – Oreos

toys – Legos

books – Go, Dog, Go

•••••••••••••••••••••   **LESSON 36**   •••••••••••••••••••••

Story narration: "The Hen and the Golden Eggs"
Poem review: "Hearts Are Like Doors" (Lesson 27) and
"Days of the Week" (Lesson 35)

Note to Instructor: *Review "Hearts Are Like Doors" and "Days of the Week" today. Then read aloud the Aesop's Fable below.*

Read the following Aesop's Fable aloud to the student, and then ask the "starter questions" at the end of the story. Remember to encourage the student to answer in complete sentences. Then ask the student, "What is the one thing you remember from the story?" Write his answer down and read it back to him.

The Hen and the Golden Eggs

A man and his wife once had a hen which laid a little golden egg for them every day. They took good care of the hen, petted her, and fed her well. Every morning they would say to her, "Thank you, little hen, for your gift!" And every evening they would feed her a hot mash and say, "Sleep well, little hen!"

Finally, they saved enough golden eggs to build a nice little cottage in the forest. Then the little hen provided them with enough gold to buy food and clothes and to share with others who needed help. For many years, they were thankful to have the little hen with them.

But the more they had, the greedier they became! One day, the man said to his wife, "Why are we waiting to get one little egg of gold each day? Our hen must have lots of golden eggs inside her. Let's kill her and look! Then we can have all of the gold at once. We will be even richer!"

So the greedy man and his wife killed the hen and cut her open. But they were shocked to discover that the little hen was no different inside from other chickens. Day by day, they grew poorer without the eggs from the little hen. By trying to become rich all at once, they lost the only source of gold they had.

Moral: If you are greedy and harm others to get more, you may lose what you have.

Note to Instructor: *Use these questions to help the student summarize the story.*

Instructor: Who owned the hen?
Student: *The farmer and his wife owned the hen.*

Instructor: What was so special about the hen?
Student: *She could lay golden eggs.*

Instructor: How did the farmer and his wife spend the gold?
Student: *They bought food [and clothes and helped other people].*

Instructor: After a while, what did they do to the hen?
Student: *They killed the hen.*

Instructor: Why did they kill the hen?
Student: *They were greedy and they wanted all the gold that they thought was inside her.*

Instructor: Did the farmer find gold inside the hen?
Student: *No, the hen was just like every other hen.*

Instructor: According to the moral of the story, what happens to those who harm others to get more?
Student: *They lose everything they have.*

•   **LESSON 37**   • • • • • • • • • • • • • • • • • • •

Nouns (Identifying nouns in a story)
Poem review: "Hearts Are Like Doors" (Lesson 27)
and "Days of the Week" (Lesson 35)

Note to Instructor: *Review "Hearts Are Like Doors" and "Days of the Week" today.*

The student will need drawing supplies for the enrichment activity.

Instructor: Say the definition of a noun with me.

TOGETHER: **A noun is the name of a person, place, thing, or idea.**

Instructor: I am going to read the story about the hen to you again, stopping at the end of each sentence. Tell me the words you hear that name persons, places, or things.

Note to Instructor: *Have the student watch you run your finger under each word as you read. Stop at the end of each sentence and help the student find the nouns. If the student has trouble finding the nouns, encourage the student to listen for these words by pausing briefly when you say them. At this time, don't be concerned if the student does not name the nouns "morning," "evening," "years," and "day," since these are not concrete "things" that the student can see.*

- Paragraph 1: Man, wife, hen, egg, day, hen, morning, hen, gift, evening, mash, hen.
- Paragraph 2: Eggs, cottage, forest, hen, gold, food, clothes, years, hen.
- Paragraph 3: Day, man, wife, egg, gold, hen, eggs, gold.
- Paragraph 4: Man, wife, hen, hen, chickens, day, day, eggs, hen, gold.

Enrichment Activity

On one sheet of paper, have the student draw small pictures of nouns in the story. Label each little drawing, and title the picture "Nouns."

· **LESSON 38** · · · · · · · · · · · · · · · · · ·

Proper nouns (Days of the week)

Note to Instructor: *The instructor will need a pencil and paper for this lesson. The student will need a pencil, paper, and drawing supplies for the enrichment activity.*

Instructor: Let's say the names of the days of the week together three times.

TOGETHER (three times): Sunday, Monday, Tuesday, Wednesday, Thursday, Friday, Saturday.

Instructor: I am going to write down each of these names of the days of the week. See, each one begins with a capital letter. Now, I am going to make a list of things we do each day.

Note to Instructor: *If your family doesn't have a regular schedule, make a schedule for one special week. You may wish to post a schedule each week somewhere the student can see, so he will begin to see a family routine. Children find comfort in routine.*

Enrichment Activity

The student may make his own personal schedule by writing the names of the days of the week and drawing pictures for each day.

•••••••••••••••••••• **LESSON 39** ••••••••••••••••••••

Addresses
Common and proper nouns (Aunts and uncles)
Poem review: "The Caterpillar" (Lesson 2)
and "Days of the Week" (Lesson 35)

Note to Instructor: *The instructor will need a pencil and paper for this lesson. The student will need a pencil and an envelope for the enrichment activity.*

Review "The Caterpillar" and "Days of the Week" today. You will need the address of an aunt or uncle for this lesson.

Instructor: Our address tells people where we live. What is our address?

Note to Instructor: *Write the address with ZIP code as the student dictates it to you. If the student is unsure of his address and ZIP code, repeat it five times together.*

Instructor: Let's look at another address together. This is the address of your uncle/aunt. Can you show me the ZIP code?

Note to Instructor: *Write the sentence "My aunt/uncle lives in (city, state)" while the student watches.*

Instructor: Remember, the words "uncle" and "aunt" could name anyone's uncle or aunt, so those words are not written with a capital letter. They are common nouns. But the name of a particular uncle or aunt is their proper name and it is written with a capital letter. Let us name particular uncles and aunts, and I will write their names for you.

Note to Instructor: *Write out these sentences, following the examples below.*

My mother's brother is Uncle _____.

My mother's sister is Aunt _____.

My father's brother is Uncle _____.

My father's sister is Aunt _____.

_____

Enrichment Activity

The student may copy his own address on an envelope and mail himself something! Copying an entire address is daunting for many first graders; only do this activity if the student is writing easily.

······· **LESSON 40** ·······

Proper nouns (Months of the year)
Oral usage: "See/Saw/Seen"
Poem review: "Days of the Week" (Lesson 35)

Note to Instructor: *The instructor will need a highlighter marker and calendar for the lesson. The student will need a pencil and paper for the enrichment activity.*

Review "Days of the Week" today.

Instructor: We have learned that each day of the week has a name. The months of the year also have names. There are twelve months in each year. Listen while I say the names: January, February, March, April, May, June, July, August, September, October, November, December.

Note to Instructor: *Give the student a calendar to browse and identify the names of the months. He can use a marker to circle the names.*

Instructor: Let's say the first three months together, three times. Remember, those months are January, February, March.

TOGETHER (three times): January, February, March.

Instructor: Now let's do the next three: April, May, June.

TOGETHER (three times): April, May, June.

Instructor: Now the next three: July, August, September.

TOGETHER (three times): July, August, September.

Instructor: And now the last three: October, November, December.

TOGETHER (three times): October, November, December.

Oral Usage Exercise

Note to Instructor: *"See" is the present tense of "to see." "Saw" is the past tense. "Seen" is also a past form of "to see," but must always be used with the helping verb "has" or "have."*

Instructor: Repeat these sentences after me. "I saw a bluebird in June."
Student: *I saw a bluebird in June.*

Instructor: "I have seen many birds in the summer."
Student: *I have seen many birds in the summer.*

Instructor: "I saw snow in January."
Student: *I saw snow in January.*

Instructor: "I have seen snow many times before."
Student: *I have seen snow many times before.*

Instructor: "He saw beautiful flowers in April."
Student: *He saw beautiful flowers in April.*

Instructor: "He has seen tulips bloom in March."
Student: *He has seen tulips bloom in March.*

Instructor: "Have you seen red leaves in the fall?"
Student: *Have you seen red leaves in the fall?*

Instructor: "Yes, I have seen beautiful red and yellow leaves."
Student: *Yes, I have seen beautiful red and yellow leaves.*

Enrichment Activity

The spelling and pronunciation of "February" is difficult. Although dictionaries give acceptable pronunciations that leave out the sound of the first "r", you may wish to emphasize this syllable ("feb-**roo**-air-ee") as a game. This exercise will help prevent misspelling when writing "February." Have the student practice copying "February" and then spelling it from memory.

LESSON 41

Proper nouns (Months of the year)
Poem review: "Days of the Week" (Lesson 35)

Note to Instructor: *Review "Days of the Week" today.*

The instructor will need a pen and a calendar for this lesson as well as paper and scissors for the enrichment activity.

Instructor: I am going to say the months of the year: January, February, March, April, May, June, July, August, September, October, November, December. Let's practice again saying those months.

Instructor: Let's say the first three months together, three times. Remember, those months are January, February, March.

TOGETHER (three times): January, February, March.

Instructor: Now let's do the next three: April, May, June.

TOGETHER (three times): April, May, June.

Instructor: Now the next three: July, August, September.

TOGETHER (three times): July, August, September.

Instructor: And now the last three: October, November, December.

TOGETHER (three times): October, November, December.

Instructor: Now let's look at a calendar together and find out what months are birthday months for our family.

Note to Instructor: *Get a calendar and mark the birthdays of each person in the family. Mark the holidays your family celebrates. Give the student his own calendar, if possible, and mark for him birthdays and special holidays your family celebrates.*

Enrichment Activity

Copy two lists of the months in order, skipping a line between each month. Have the student cut apart one list, mix up the months, and rearrange them in order, using the uncut list to self-check.

·   **LESSON 42**   · · · · · · · · · · · · · · · · · · ·

Introducing copywork sentences: "My name"

Note to Instructor: *The student will need a pencil and paper.*

By doing copywork, the student learns the look and feel of a correctly composed sentence that is properly spelled, spaced, and punctuated. Copywork engages both the visual and motor memory of a student. It gives the student correct models while he is still struggling with the basics of writing conventions: spaces between words, capital letters, punctuation, and spelling. In the beginning, it is helpful for some children to say the word aloud, sounding it out as they copy. You may wish to write out the copywork in your own handwriting for the student to see. Sit beside the student and correct him when he begins to copy incorrectly, rather than waiting until he is finished.

Instructor: Today we are going to start copying sentences, so that you can practice writing. We will also practice leaving proper spaces between words.

Note to Instructor: *Three options will be given for each copywork. Choose the appropriate length for the student's skill. If the student lives in a "blended" family, use your discretion and substitute your own sentence for the third option.*

My name is_____. (student's first name)

My full name is_____. (student's full name)

Family members have the same last name. My family name is _____.

_____

Enrichment Activity

Copy names of family members that the student may not already write easily.

························   **LESSON 43**   ·····················

Poem memorization: "The Months"
Copywork: "My birthday"

Note to Instructor: *The student will need a pencil and paper.*

Read the poem aloud to the student three times now. Repeat this triple reading twice more during the day.

Instructor: The months are not the same length! Some months have more days than others. Most have 30 or 31 days, but February has only 28. And February is even stranger—once every four years February has one more day added. We call this year "Leap Year." I will read you a poem that will help you remember the number of days in each month. Remember that "four and twenty-four" is the same as "twenty-eight"!

The Months
Mother Goose rhyme

> Thirty days hath September,
> April, June, and November;
> All the rest have thirty-one,
> Except for February alone,
> Which has four and twenty-four
> Till leap year gives it one day more.

Instructor: Now let's practice the poem together.

Together (three times): Thirty days hath September,
April, June, and November.

Together (three times): All the rest have thirty-one,
Except for February alone.

Together (three times): Which has four and twenty-four
Till leap year gives it one day more.

Note to Instructor: *If the student inquires, an explanation might be given: Leap years were added to the calendar to make the calendar match the movement of the earth around the sun.*

Copywork

Choose appropriate length for the student's ability:

_____

(copy month of student's birthday)

My birthday is in _____ .
                          (month)

I have cake on my birthday in _____ .
                                                  (month)

Nouns (Ideas)
Copywork: "Love"
Poem review: "The Months" (Lesson 43)

Note to Instructor: *The student will need a pencil and paper.*

Repeat the poem "The Months" three times along with the student before beginning today's lesson.

Instructor: Say the definition of a noun with me three times.

TOGETHER (three times): **A noun is the name of a person, place, thing, or idea.**

Instructor: An idea is something you think about in your mind, but cannot see or touch—like love, anger, energy, loneliness, or fear. You can name ideas, but you can't see them.

Note to Instructor: *Read the following sentences aloud to the student. Move your finger under the words as you read, so the student can see the words. The underlined words are names for ideas.*

The puppy gives me his <u>love</u>.

I felt <u>anger</u> when the boy teased my puppy.

I am full of <u>energy</u> when I get a good night's sleep.

<u>Kindness</u> makes people happy together.

There was no <u>peace</u> between the cat and the dog.

<u>Loneliness</u> comes when everyone leaves me.

Instructor: Can you see love? Can you see energy? No, but these are things that you feel and think about. They are ideas. Even though you can't see them, they are real. These idea words are nouns.

Copywork

Choose appropriate length for the student:

I feel love for you.

My mother feels love for me.

The people in my family feel love for each other.

······· **LESSON 45** ········

Noun review
Copywork: "Four types of nouns"
Poem review: "The Months" (Lesson 43)

Note to Instructor: *Both the instructor and the student will need a pencil and paper.*

Review "The Months" today.

Instructor: Let's review the definition of a noun.

TOGETHER (three times):   **A noun is the name of a person, place, thing, or idea.**

Instructor: Remember, common nouns name persons that could be lots of different people—like "doctors," "brothers," "uncles," or "teachers." But proper nouns name special, particular people. Let's name some common nouns for persons and then name special, particular persons.

Note to Instructor: *Help the student think of the proper names for uncles, aunts, teachers, doctors, ministers, or baby-sitters.*

Instructor: Remember, common nouns name places that could be lots of different places, but proper nouns name special, particular places like Plains, Arizona. Let's name some common nouns for places and then give a special, particular name for those kinds of places.

Note to Instructor: *Help the student think of the proper names for towns, rivers, mountains, stores, restaurants, ice-cream shops, etc.*

Instructor: Now, let us name some common nouns for things and then give a special particular name for those things.

Note to Instructor: *Help the student to think of proper nouns for toys, songs, poems, cars, tractors, or books.*

Instructor: What are some words that name ideas? We will only talk about common nouns for these. Today we will name those idea words that we think about in our mind, or feel, but can't see or touch like a thing can be felt or touched. Do you remember some we named in the last lesson? (Love, anger, energy, kindness, peace, loneliness.)

Note to Instructor: *Feelings are the most immediate "ideas" for most young children. Help the student identify other feelings. If you think that he will understand, you can also discuss freedom, obedience, responsibility, patience, diligence, and other character qualities. These, too, are ideas.*

Copywork

Today the student will write some nouns of each kind. Title a sheet of paper "Nouns." Divide the paper into four horizontal sections, and title the sections "Persons," "Places," "Things," and "Ideas." Ask the student to think of a noun to go in each section. You write each word on another piece of paper, and ask the student to copy it onto his "Nouns" sheet. He should have at least one noun to go in each section.

Enrichment Activity

The student may add words to the list, as many as appropriate for his writing ability.

························ **LESSON 46** ······················

Introducing pronouns (I, me, my, mine)
Oral usage: "Ordering 'I' and 'me'"
Poem review: "The Months" (Lesson 43)

Note to Instructor: *Review "The Months" today.*

We will be covering these pronouns over the next five lessons. For your reference, here is the full list covered:

> *I, me, my, mine;*
> *you, your, yours;*
> *he, she, him, her, it, his, hers, its;*
> *we, us, our, ours;*
> *they, them, their, theirs.*

Instructor: **A pronoun is a word used in the place of a noun.** Try to say the definition with me as I repeat it three times.

TOGETHER: **A pronoun is a word used in the place of a noun.**

Instructor: We have learned that **a noun names a person, place, thing, or idea.** Your own name is a noun. Today, we are going to talk about pronouns that can take the place of your name. These pronouns are "I, me, my, mine." Let's repeat those together three times.

TOGETHER (three times): I, me, my, mine.

Instructor: What is your name?
Student: *My name is _____ .*

Instructor: Instead of saying "(Student's name) went out to play," you could say, "I went out to play." Repeat those two sentences for me.
Student: *[Student's name] went out to play. I went out to play.*

Instructor: The pronouns that stand for you are "I, me, my, mine." We just used "I." Now let's use "me." Instead of saying, "Please give (student's name) a cookie," you could say, "Please give me a cookie." Repeat those two sentences for me.
Student: *Please give [student's name] a cookie. Please give me a cookie.*

Instructor: Now let's practice using "my." Instead of saying, "That is (student's name)'s toothbrush, you could say, "That is my toothbrush." Repeat those two sentences for me.
Student: *That is [student's name]'s toothbrush. That is my toothbrush.*

Instructor   Now we have used "I," "me," "my." Let's use "mine." Instead of saying, "That towel is (student's name)'s," you could say, "That towel is mine." Repeat those two sentences for me.

Student: *That towel is [student's name]'s. That towel is mine.*

Instructor: I am going to say the definition of a pronoun again: **A pronoun is a word used in the place of a noun.** Say it with me again.

TOGETHER: **A pronoun is a word used in the place of a noun.**

Instructor: Now say the pronouns that can be used in place of your own name when you speak of yourself. We used them in sentences today: "I, me, my, mine."

TOGETHER: I, me, my, mine.

Oral Usage Exercise

Instructor: When you are speaking of yourself and another person, always speak of the other person first. Say, "Charlie and I went fishing," not "I and Charlie went fishing." Repeat these sentences after me:

Jane and I are going with Mom.

My sister and I played soccer.

My father and I went to town.

Instructor: Say, "My mother drove Ellen and me to town," not "My mother drove me and Ellen to town." Here is a trick to help you remember: If you say "me" first, it will sound like "mean" Ellen! Repeat these sentences after me.

My sister invited Joy and me to her doll tea party.

The clown did a juggling trick for Lee and me.

My mother took my brother and me shopping.

······················ **LESSON 47** ······················

Pronouns (You, your, yours)
Copywork: "Pronoun list 1"
Poem review: "The Months" (Lesson 43)

Note to Instructor: *Both the instructor and the student will need a pencil and paper.*

Review "The Months" today.

Instructor: Let's say the definition of a **pronoun** together three times.

TOGETHER: **A pronoun is a word used in the place of a noun.**

Instructor: Do you remember the pronouns that speak of yourself?
Student: *Yes, they are "I, me, my, mine."*

Instructor: Let's say those together three times.

TOGETHER (three times): I, me, my, mine.

Instructor: There are also pronouns that can take the place of the person to whom you are speaking. These pronouns are "you, your, yours." Let's say those together three times.

TOGETHER (three times): You, your, yours.

Instructor: Instead of saying, "(Instructor's name) is here with me," you can say, "You are here with me." Repeat those two sentences for me.
Student: *[Instructor's name] is here with me. You are here with me.*

Instructor: Instead of saying, "This is (instructor's name)'s book," you can say, "This is your book." Repeat those two sentences for me.
Student: *This is [instructor's name]'s book. This is your book.*

Instructor: Instead of saying, "This pencil is (instructor's name)'s," you can say, "This pencil is yours." Repeat those two sentences for me.
Student: *This pencil is [instructor's name]'s. This pencil is yours.*

Instructor: The pronouns "you," "your," and "yours" take the place of another person's name.

Copywork

Today the student will begin to make his own list of pronouns. Title a sheet of paper "Pronouns." Then write out in your own handwriting the two lists of pronouns we have learned: "I, me, my, mine" and "you, your, yours." Because the student has not learned commas, write these in vertical lists. Ask the student to copy these vertical lists of pronouns onto his own paper.

········· · · · · · ·   **LESSON 48**   ·····················

Pronouns (He, she, him, her, it, his, hers, its)
Copywork: "Pronoun list 2"
Poem review: "The Months" (Lesson 43)

Note to Instructor: *Both the instructor and the student will need a pencil and paper.*

Review "The Months" today.

Instructor: Let's say the definition of a **pronoun** together three times.

TOGETHER (three times): **A pronoun is a word used in the place of a noun**.

Instructor: We have learned that "I, me, my, mine" can be used in place of your own name. Let's say those together.

TOGETHER: I, me, my mine.

Instructor: We have learned that "you, your, yours" can be used in place of the name of someone to whom you are speaking. Let's say those together.

TOGETHER: You, your, yours.

Instructor: Now let's talk about the pronouns "he, she, him, her, it, his, hers, its." Can you say those with me, three times?

TOGETHER (three times): He, she, him, her, it, his, hers, its.

Instructor: Instead of saying to you, "Jim is coming," I could say "He is coming." Repeat those two sentences for me.

Student: *Jim is coming. He is coming.*

Instructor: Instead of saying "Sara likes dessert," I could say "She likes dessert." Repeat those two sentences for me.

Student: *Sara likes dessert. She likes dessert.*

Instructor: Instead of saying "Wait for Ron," I could say, "Wait for him." Repeat those two sentences for me.

Student: *Wait for Ron. Wait for him.*

Instructor: Instead of saying, "I gave a cookie to Kim," I could say, "I gave a cookie to her." Repeat those two sentences for me.

Student: *I gave a cookie to Kim. I gave a cookie to her.*

Instructor: Instead of saying, "Bob found a worm," I could say, "Bob found it." Repeat those two sentences for me.

Student: *Bob found a worm. Bob found it.*

Instructor: Instead of saying, "This is Bob's pet worm," I could say, "This is his pet worm." Repeat those two sentences for me.

Student: *This is Bob's pet worm. This is his pet worm.*

Instructor: Instead of saying, "This strawberry shortcake is Lori's," I could say, "This strawberry shortcake is hers." Repeat those two sentences for me.

Student: *This strawberry shortcake is Lori's. This strawberry shortcake is hers.*

Instructor: Instead of saying, "The cat's bed is soft," I could say, "Its bed is soft." Repeat those two sentences for me.

Student: *The cat's bed is soft. Its bed is soft.*

Copywork

Today the student will continue making his list of pronouns. Write out the pronouns "he, she, him, her, it, his, hers, its" in a vertical list. Ask the student to copy these pronouns onto his "Pronouns" page. If the list is too long for the student to do at one sitting, have him do half in the morning and half in the evening (or complete the list yourself while the student watches).

························ LESSON 49 ······················

Pronouns (We, us, our, ours)
Copywork: "Pronoun list 3"
Poem review: "The Months" (Lesson 43)

Note to Instructor: *Both the instructor and the student will need a pencil and paper.*
Review "The Months" today.

Instructor: Let's say the definition of a **pronoun** together.

TOGETHER: **A pronoun is a word used in the place of a noun.**

Instructor: Here are the pronouns we learned in the first two pronoun lessons: "I, me, my, mine, you, your, yours." Let's say those together three times.

TOGETHER (three times): I, me, my, mine, you, your, yours.

Instructor: Now let's review the pronouns we learned in the last lesson: "he, she, him, her, it, his, hers, its." Let's say those together three times.

TOGETHER (three times): He, she, him, her, it, his, hers, its.

Instructor: Today we are going to say and write pronouns that mean more than one person. Those pronouns are "we, us, our, ours." Let's say that together three times.

TOGETHER (three times): We, us, our, ours.

Instructor: Imagine that you and a person like cookies. Can you tell me that both of you like cookies? Start with "We..."
Student: *We like cookies.*

Instructor: Now ask me for some cookies for both of you. Start your sentence with, "Please give..."
Student: *Please give us some cookies.*

Instructor: If I give cookies to both of you, whose cookies are they? Start your sentence with, "The cookies are..."
Student: *The cookies are our cookies.*

Instructor: Whose cookies are they? Start with, "They are..."
Student: *They are ours.*

Instructor: "We, us, our, ours" are pronouns. They take the place of the nouns that named you and the other person.

Copywork

Write out the pronouns "we, us, our, ours" in a vertical list. Ask the student to copy these pronouns onto his "Pronouns" page.

.... **LESSON 50** ....

Pronouns (They, them, their, theirs)
Copywork: "Pronoun list 4"

Note to the Instructor: *Both the instructor and the student will need a pencil and paper.*

Instructor: Let's say the definition of a **pronoun** together three times.

TOGETHER: **A pronoun is a word used in the place of a noun.**

Instructor: These pronouns are also used in place of nouns that mean more than one person: "they, them, their, theirs." You use them when you are talking about a group of people that does not include you! Let's say "they, them, their, theirs" together three times.

TOGETHER (three times): They, them, their, theirs.

Instructor: Together, we'll read a sentence with a noun in it. Then you choose a pronoun—"they," "them," or "their"—to use in place of the noun. "Ducks swim on the pond." What pronoun can you use in place of "ducks"?

Student: *They swim on the pond.*

Note to Instructor: *If the student is unsure of the answer, read the pronouns to him and allow him to choose.*

Instructor: "We feed the ducks." What pronoun can go in the place of "ducks"?
Student: *We feed them.*

Instructor: "I like to watch ducks swim." Can you put a pronoun in place of "ducks"?
Student: *I like to watch them swim.*

Instructor: "Ducks' feet paddle fast." What pronoun can you use for "ducks"?
Student: *Their feet paddle fast.*

Instructor: "The ducklings belong to the mother and father ducks." What pronoun can you use for "mother and father ducks"?
Student: *The ducklings belong to them.*

Instructor: Now let's review all of our pronouns! Say them after me. I, me, my, mine.
Student: *I, me, my, mine.*

Instructor: You, your, yours.

Student: *You, your, yours.*

Instructor: He, she, him, her, it, his, hers, its.
Student: *He, she, him, her, it, his, hers, its.*

Instructor: We, us, our, ours.
Student: *We, us, our, ours.*

Instructor: They, them, their, theirs.
Student: *They, them, their, theirs.*

Copywork

Write out the pronouns "they, them, their, theirs" in a vertical list. Ask the student to copy these pronouns onto his "Pronoun" page.

· ·　**LESSON 51**　· ·

Story narration: "The Bundle of Sticks"

Note to Instructor: *Read the following Aesop's Fable aloud to the student, and then ask the "starter questions" at the end of the story. Remember to encourage the student to answer in complete sentences. Then ask the student, "What is the one thing you remember from the story?" Write his answer down and read it back to him.*

The Bundle of Sticks

A father had a family of six children: three boys and three girls.

They were very noisy children, for they spent most of each day quarrelling with each other. That day, the house was particularly noisy.

Jacob was angry with Emily for eating the last piece of toast.

"You already had two pieces of toast and I only had one piece. It is not fair!" he complained.

"You always get whatever you want, Jacob. You never leave anything for the rest of us!" she yelled back.

Sally stamped her feet because Martha was playing with Sally's favorite doll. "You have the doll I always play with! You know that she is my favorite, Martha! I refuse to play dolls with you if you keep taking the best doll!"

"Well, I don't want to play dolls with you anyway," Martha shouted back. "You are so bossy!"

Eric yelled at Simon because Simon was humming the same tune over and over again. "I am trying to read," Eric complained, "and you are humming just to annoy me. Stop humming, or I am going to tell Dad!"

Simon gave Eric a mean look. "I will do whatever I want to do," he snapped. "You are not Mom or Dad. You can't tell me what to do!"

The children's father was sad that his children could not get along. So he told them to come outside into their front yard. He asked each of them to pick up a few sticks and bring them to him. He tied all of the sticks into one bundle and gave the bundle to Eric. "Try to break it in half," he commanded.

Eric tried with all his might, but he could not break the bundle.

The father gave the bundle of sticks to Martha, but she could not break it, either. Each of the six children tried to break the bundle, but they could not.

Then the father untied the bundle and divided the sticks among his children. "Now try to break the sticks one by one," he ordered.

The children easily snapped the sticks in half.

"Children," their father said, "do you not see that when you agree with each other and get along together, our family will be impossible to break apart? The bundle of all the sticks was impossible to break. But the single sticks were easy to snap. When you argue and bicker and quarrel, you will be weak, like the single sticks. We cannot have a strong, happy family if each one of you is selfish and looks out only for his own interests. You must learn to agree with each other and help each other so that we may have a strong family. If you continue to fight and quarrel, you will be weak like one single stick."

Instructor: What made the father sad?
Student: *His children were quarrelling with each other.*

Instructor: What kinds of things were the brothers and sisters arguing about?
Student: *They were arguing about toys, food, and humming.*

Instructor: What did the father ask his children to pick up once they were in the yard?
Student: *The father asked the children to pick up sticks.*

Instructor: What did the father do with the sticks?
Student: *He tied them into a bundle.*

Instructor: What did the father ask the children to do with the bundle?
Student: *He asked them to break it.*

Instructor: Were the children able to break the single sticks?
Student: *Yes, the children were able to break the single sticks.*

Instructor: What was the father trying to teach his children by having them try to break the bundle of sticks?
Student: *He was trying to teach them that they would be stronger if they agreed with each other instead of fighting.*

•••••••••••••••••••• **LESSON 52** ••••••••••••••••••••

Introducing verbs (Action verbs)
Poem review: "Work" (Lesson 15)

Note to Instructor: *Review "Work" today.*

It isn't necessary for the student to understand state of being, linking, or helping verbs while memorizing this definition—those will be covered at a later date.

The student will need a pencil and paper for the enrichment activity.

Instructor: We have talked for many lessons about nouns, which name people, places, things, or ideas. We have talked about pronouns, which can be used in the place of nouns. Today we are going to talk about words that tell us what those nouns and pronouns do! Those words are called **verbs**. I will read the definition of a verb aloud to you three times.

Instructor (three times): A verb is a word that does an action, shows a state of being, links two words together, or helps another verb.

Instructor: We will talk about action verbs today. I am going to say some words that are action words: "walk," "stoop," "run," "laugh," "write," "erase," "cry," "skip," "throw," "catch," "dance," and "eat." These are all verbs. Can you think of more actions?

Note to Instructor: *After the student tells you the ones he can think of, read the following list to him:*

Run, skip, roll, fall, jump, eat, sing, sleep, jump, skate, talk, read, kick, hit, crawl, hop, bark, dance, play, look, paint, climb, swing, float, fly, open, close, move, race, smell, shout, yell, laugh, clean, squeak, mew, roar, growl.

Instructor: Tell me as many of these action verbs as you can remember.
Student: *(repeats as many verbs as possible)*

Instructor: Remember, **a verb is a word that does an action**. Let's say that part of the definition together three times.

Together (three times): **A verb is a word that does an action.**

Enrichment Activity

The student can title a sheet of paper "Action Verbs," and make a list of as many action verbs as he can remember. He can illustrate the list if he chooses. He can also add to the list at any time.

•••••••••••••••••••••   **LESSON 53**   •••••••••••••••••••

Pronouns

Action verbs

Copywork: "Label nouns and verbs 1"

Note to Instructor: *The student will need a pencil and paper.*

Read the student the following list of pronouns three times. If the student can chime in with any of the pronouns, encourage him to do so, but he does not need to memorize the lists.

I, me, my, mine;
you, your, yours;
he, she, him, her, it, his, hers, its;
we, us, our, ours;
they, them, their, theirs.

Instructor: I am going to say the definition of a verb three times for you.

Instructor (three times): A verb is a word that does an action, shows a state of being, links two words together, or helps another verb.

Instructor: Now I want you to repeat parts of this definition after me: **A verb is a word that does an action.**

Student: *A verb is a word that does an action.*

Instructor: Now listen to the second part of the definition: **Shows a state of being.** Repeat that for me.

Student: *Shows a state of being.*

Instructor: Links two words together.

Student: *Links two words together.*

Instructor: Or helps another verb.

Student: *Or helps another verb.*

Instructor: We are going to practice using action verbs now. You name some family members. These names are nouns. Now think up action verbs for each family member. What can you imagine each person doing? For example, "The baby crawls." Say the sentences out loud and act out the action.

Note to Instructor: *Suggest these verbs if the student has trouble coming up with his own: eats, drinks, sips, crawls, cries, swings, runs, walks, washes, works, laughs, drives, swims, yells, paints.*

Copywork

Choose one of the following sentences of appropriate length for the student's ability. After he copies the sentence, tell him to print an "N" above the nouns and a "V" above the verbs in each sentence he copies.

Rabbit ran the race.

Ben and Sherri skipped and hopped.

The wind howled and the rain blew and the thunder roared.

Enrichment Activity

The student may add more verbs to his "Action Verbs" sheet started in Lesson 52.

∙∙∙∙∙∙∙∙∙∙∙∙∙∙∙∙∙∙∙∙∙   **LESSON 54**   ∙∙∙∙∙∙∙∙∙∙∙∙∙∙∙∙∙∙∙∙∙

Telephone numbers
Addresses
Poem review: "Hearts Are Like Doors" (Lesson 27)

Note to Instructor: *Review "Hearts Are Like Doors" today.*

If the student already knows his home telephone number, do the enrichment activity below in place of the lesson.

The student may need a new address book and a pencil for the enrichment activity.

Instructor: Today, I want to be sure that you know what our family's home telephone number is. Our telephone number has ten numbers in it. The first three numbers are the area code. Our area code is _____. Say that with me three times.

TOGETHER (three times): (area code)

Instructor: An "area" is a certain amount of space. So the "area code" for our telephone is the same for a lot of people in the space near where we live. All telephone numbers from our area have the same first three numbers, but we have a telephone number at our home that no one else has! Our personal family telephone number has seven numbers. Those numbers are ___-____. Say that with me three times.

TOGETHER (three times): (telephone number)

Instructor: Our whole telephone number is (area code)____-_____. We are going to say that together today TEN times! Let's hold up our fingers and fold one down every time say the number.

TOGETHER (ten times): (telephone number)

Instructor: Never give your telephone number to strangers, or give it out on the computer. Never, never, never! If someone asks for your telephone number, say, "Ask my parents!" Now, let's review who you are and where you live. What is your full name?

Student: *[Student gives first, middle, and last name.]*

Instructor: Where do you live?

Student: *[Student gives address. Encourage him to add the ZIP code.]*

Instructor: What is your telephone number?

Student: *[Student gives full telephone number.]*

Enrichment Activity

Have the student learn telephone numbers of trusted family members, neighbors, or friends. The student may start an address book with approved addresses and/or telephone numbers in it.

•••••••••••••••••••••   **LESSON 55**   •••••••••••••••••••

Nouns
Pronouns
Action verbs
Copywork: "Label nouns and verbs 2"

Note to Instructor: *The student will need a pencil and paper.*

Read the student the following list of pronouns three times. He does not need to memorize the list now, but encourage him to chime in.

I, me, my, mine;
you, your, yours;
he, she, him, her, it, his, hers, its;
we, us, our, ours;
they, them, their, theirs.

Instructor: Say the definition of a **noun** with me.

TOGETHER: **A noun is the name of a person, place, thing, or idea.**

Instructor: I will repeat the definition of a verb for you. **A verb is a word that does an action, shows a state of being, links two words together, or helps another verb.** Let's repeat the first part of that definition together three times: **A verb is a word that does an action.**

TOGETHER (three times): **A verb is a word that does an action.**

Instructor: Today we are going to talk about nouns that name animals and the action verbs that these animals can do. Can you give me the name of any animals along with an action these animals could do? For example, "The bird soared through the sky," or "The elephant crashed through the jungle."

Note to Instructor: *Refer to verb list in Lesson 52 if needed. Allow the student to act out the action verbs. Remind him that if he can't do it, the word may not be an action verb!*

Copywork ———————————————————————————

Choose one, two, or three of the following sentences for the student to copy. Make sure that he skips a line between each sentence. After he copies the sentences, ask him to print an "N" above the nouns and a "V" above the verbs in each sentence.

The cat scratches.

The dog barks.

The hamster hides.

The lion roars.

The monkey climbs.

Enrichment Activity

The student may add more verbs to his "Action Verbs" sheet started in Lesson 52.

$\cdots\cdots\cdots\cdots\cdots\cdots\cdots$ **LESSON 56** $\cdots\cdots\cdots\cdots\cdots\cdots$

Picture narration: "A Sunday Afternoon on the Island of La Grande Jatte"

Instructor: Look carefully at the picture while I tell you about the artist, Georges-Pierre Seurat [zhorzh pyayr syu-RAH]. He was born in Paris in 1859, so he was younger than Mary Cassatt but much older than Andrew Wyeth. This painting is called "A Sunday Afternoon on the Island of La Grand Jatte [lah grhand zhot)]." It shows a lazy afternoon in the city of Paris. Georges-Pierre Seurat worked on this painting for two whole years. The original painting is nearly seven feet tall and ten feet wide! Instead of painting it with brush strokes, the artist used thousands and thousands of tiny dots, or "points," of color to make up the picture.

In the front of the picture, a man and a woman are strolling along with two animals. What kind of animals are they walking?

Student: *They are walking a dog and a monkey.*

Instructor: "Strolling" and "walking" are both verbs that describe the same kind of action. What kind of verbs are they?

Student: *They are action verbs.*

Instructor: Tell me two other actions that people are doing in the picture.

Student: *People are [sitting, eating, dancing, rowing.]*

Instructor: There is another dog in the picture. What is it doing?

Student: *The dog is eating someone's picnic!*

Instructor: Four people in the picture are carrying umbrellas. Can you point out each one?

Student: *[points]*

Instructor: In the picture, is it raining or is the sun shining?

Student: *The sun is shining.*

Instructor: How can you tell? (If necessary, help the student by pointing out the shadows.)

Student: *The picture has shadows in it.*

Instructor: What are the umbrellas protecting the people from?

Student: *They are protecting people from the sun.*

Instructor: What can you see over on the left-hand side of the picture? Hint: there are boats on it!

Student: *There is a river in the picture.*

Instructor: Do you think that it is summer or winter in the picture?

Student: *It is summer in the picture.*

Instructor: How do you know? Hint: look at the trees.

Student: *There are leaves on the trees.*

Note to Instructor: *You can view "A Sunday Afternoon on the Island of La Grande Jatte" in the online collection of the Art Institute of Chicago (www.artic.edu). Search for "Seurat" or go to http://www.artic.edu/ artaccess/AA_Impressionist/pages/IMP_7_lg.shtml.*

••••••••••••••••••••• **LESSON 57** •••••••••••••••••••

Cumulative poem review

Instructor: Today we are going to review all of the poems you have worked on so far. When we recite a poem, we begin with the title and author. I will read each poem to you, and then I want you to try to say the poem back to me. Remember: Stand up straight! Don't fidget while you're reciting! And speak in a nice, loud, slow voice.

Note to Instructor: *Read each poem to the student before asking him to repeat it. If he repeats it accurately, move on to the next poem. If he stumbles, ask him to repeat the line he cannot remember three times, and make a note to review that poem daily until it is mastered. Remind the student that "Anonymous" means we don't know who wrote the poem.*

Lesson	Poem	Author
2	"The Caterpillar"	Christina G. Rossetti
15	"Work"	Anonymous
27	"Hearts Are Like Doors"	Anonymous
35	"Days of the Week"	Mother Goose rhyme, adapted by Sara Buffington
43	"The Months"	Mother Goose rhyme

LESSON 58

Pronouns
Action verbs
Action poem: "Dancing"
Copywork: "Dancing"

Note to Instructor: *The student will need a pencil and paper for this lesson as well as drawing supplies for the enrichment activity.*

Instructor: Do you remember the definition of a noun? **A noun is the name of a person, place, thing, or idea. A pronoun is a word used in the place of a noun.** Let's say the definition of a pronoun together three times.

TOGETHER (three times): **A pronoun is a word used in the place of a noun.**

Instructor: Now I'll read you the list of pronouns that we talked about earlier. If you can say any of these along with me, jump in and say them!

    I, me, my, mine;
    you, your, yours;
    he, she, him, her, it, his, hers, its;
    we, us, our, ours;
    they, them, their, theirs.

Instructor: **A verb is a word that does an action, shows a state of being, links two words together, or helps another verb.** Let's repeat the first part of that definition three times.

TOGETHER (three times): **A verb is a word that does an action.**

Instructor: Today I'm going to read you a poem that is full of action words. I'm going to read it once for you just to listen. Then I'm going to read it again and you can do the actions while I read.

Note to Instructor: *Read the entire poem aloud while the student listens quietly. Read the poem again slowly, pausing after each action word to give time for the student to act out the motions. Technically, "hop" and "skip" are nouns in this poem, not verbs (and "up" and "down" are prepositions). But as you read, let the student act out any actions he wishes. The goal is for him to recognize action words. Distinctions between verbs and other kinds of words that might express actions will be explained in more detail when the student is older.*

Dancing[1]

Eleanor Farjeon [FAR-jun]

A hop, a skip, and off you go!
Happy heart and merry toe,
Up and down and in and out,
This way, that way, round about!
Bend like grasses in the breeze,
Wave your arms like wind-blown trees,
Dart like swallows, glide like fish,
Dance like anything you wish.
Soundless as the snowflakes white,
Swift as shooting stars at night,
Nimble as a goblin elf,
Dance, dance, and be yourself.
Stately, sprightly, so and so,
Quick and slow,
To and fro,
Kicking high and jumping low,
A skip, a hop, and off you go!

Copywork

Ask the student to copy one, two, three, or four lines from the poem, depending on his ability.

Enrichment Activity

The student may copy and illustrate any lines from the poem he wishes.

1   Originally appeared in *Sing for Your Supper* by Eleanor Farjeon.

LESSON 59

Days of the week
Action verbs
Copywork: "Days of the Week"

Note to Instructor: *Both the instructor and the student will need a pencil and paper.*

Instructor: Do you remember the names of the days of the week? I will say them for you: Sunday, Monday, Tuesday, Wednesday, Thursday, Friday, Saturday. Let's say them together.

TOGETHER: Sunday, Monday, Tuesday, Wednesday, Thursday, Friday, Saturday.

Instructor: Now I am going to read you a funny poem where members of a family are doing different things on every day of the week. It is called "Monday, Mommy Baked a Cake."

Monday, Mommy Baked a Cake

Jessie Wise

Monday, Mommy baked a cake.
Tuesday, Daddy ate a steak.
Wednesday, Brother waved, "Good-bye."
Thursday, Uncle made a pie.
Friday, Sister cooked the meat,
Then we all sat down to eat.
Saturday, we welcomed guests.
Sunday, we all took our rests.
Monday, we began anew—
The days of the week are all too few.

Instructor: Let's name something that we do on each day of the week. What do we usually do on Mondays?

Note to Instructor: *Continue through each day of the week; help the student to identify your family's routine on each day.*

Copywork

Write "Days of the Week" at the top of the student's paper. Then write out the days of the week on your own paper and ask the student to copy them. If this is too long, finish the copywork in the next lesson.

Enrichment Activity

An advanced writer may be able to write the days of the week from memory. Remind him that proper names begin with capital letters.

••••••••••••••••••••• **LESSON 60** •••••••••••••••••••

Introducing initials
Copywork: "My Initials"
Oral usage: "Pronouns"
Poem review: "The Months" (Lesson 43)

Note to Instructor: *Both the instructor and the student will need a pencil and paper.*

Review "The Months" today.

Instructor: You have learned that proper nouns begin with capital letters. The first letter of a word is its initial letter. The word "initial" means "first" or "beginning." The initial letter of a proper noun begins with a capital letter. What is the first letter of your first name?

Student: *The first letter of my first name is____.*

Instructor: That is the initial letter of your first name. What is the first letter of your middle name?

Student: *The first letter of my middle name is_____.*

Instructor: That is an initial letter also. What is the first letter of your last name?

Student: *The first letter of my last name is____.*

Instructor: That is an initial letter too. Now put those three initial letters together. These letters together are called your initials. Sometimes we use initials as a short way to refer to proper names. If I ask you to tell me your full initials, what would you say? Begin your answer with, "My initials are..."

Student: *My initials are __ __ __.*

Instructor: When we write initials, we capitalize each one. We also put a period after each initial.

Note to Instructor: *Write the student's initials for him, putting a period after each initial. Tell him that you place a period after each initial. Show the student how to make a period—just a dot, not a huge mark!*

Instructor: Now, on paper, I want you to make ten periods in a line.

Note to Instructor: *Ask the student to practice making periods.*

Copywork

Have the student copy his initials and then write them from memory.

Oral Usage Exercise

Read aloud the first sentence in each pair of sentences below. Then ask the student to substitute a pronoun for the first word (noun) in each sentence. Before beginning, read the list of pronouns to the student:

I, me, my, mine;
you, your, yours;
he, she, him, her, it, his, hers, its;
we, us, our, ours;
they, them, their, theirs.

Instructor: Mary eats cake.
Student: *She eats cake.*

Instructor: Ed is seven years old.
Student: *He is seven years old.*

Instructor: Ducks like to eat crumbs.
Student: *They like to eat crumbs.*

Instructor: The airplane took off with a roar.
Student: *It took off with a roar.*

Enrichment Activity

Talk about the full names and initials of parents. Ask the student to copy or write these initials.

• **LESSON 61** •

Initials
Identifying pronouns in a story
Oral Usage: "It is I"

Note to Instructor: *Both the instructor and the student will need a pencil and paper.*

Turn back to Lesson 51 and re-read "The Bundle of Sticks" aloud. Ask the student to follow along if he is able. Stop at the end of each sentence and ask the student to identify the pronouns (see key below). Use your discretion; it isn't necessary to read the entire story if the student's attention span is short.

Paragraph 1: [no pronouns]

Paragraph 2: they, they

Paragraph 3: [no pronouns]

Paragraph 4: you, I, it, he

Paragraph 5: you, you, you, us, she

Paragraph 6: her, you, I, you, she, my, I, you, you

Paragraph 7: I, you, you

Paragraph 8: I, you, me, I

Paragraph 9: I, I, he, you, you, me

Paragraph 10: his, he, them, their, he, them, them, him, he, it, he

Paragraph 11: his, he

Paragraph 12: she, it, they

Paragraph 13: his, he

Paragraph 14: their, you, you, our, you, you, we, you, his, you, we, you, you

Instructor: In the last lesson, we learned that the first letter of a word is its initial letter. The word "initial" means "first" or "beginning." When you write the first letter of your name instead of the whole name, you are writing your initials. Can you tell me the initials of your first, middle, and last name? Begin your sentence, "My initials are…"

Student: *My initials are ___ ___ ___.*

Instructor: Sometimes people use initials for their first and middle names only, and use the full spelling of their last name. If you were to use the initials of your first and middle names along with your full last name, how would you say your name? Begin your sentence, "My name is…"

Student: *My name is [initial][initial][last name].*

Note to Instructor: *Prompt student, if necessary.*

Instructor: Let's talk about the initials of the other members of our family.

Note to Instructor: *Talk to the student about the names and initials of members of the family. Let the student see you write the initials and last names for three people in your family. Point out the period after each initial.*

Copywork

The student will copy his own initials, using periods.

Oral Usage Exercise

Note to Instructor: *The subject pronouns "I," "he," and "she" should always be used in the sentence pattern, "It is…" or "This is…." The student should never say, "It is me!" or "It is him!" Read the following dialogue with the student, encouraging him to use the pronouns "I," "he," and "she."*

Instructor: I am going to ask you several questions. Answer them using the pronouns "I," "he," or "she." Who is there? Begin your answer with, "It is…"
Student: *It is I.*

Instructor: Is that your brother? Begin your answer with, "It is…"
Student: *It is he.*

Instructor: Is that your mother? Begin your answer with, "It is…"
Student: *It is she.*

Instructor: Let's pretend that you're knocking on the door. Go knock on it! Now I will say, "Who is it?" What will you answer?
Student: *It is I.*

Instructor: Now I'll go knock on the door! You are going to ask, "Who is it?"
Student: *Who is it?*

Instructor: It is I!

Enrichment Activity

If the student is writing easily, have him copy or write his name using initials and last name. Copy initials and last names for three other people in your family.

· **LESSON 62** ·

Story narration: "The Crow and the Pitcher"

Note to Instructor: *Read the following Aesop's Fable aloud to the student, and then ask the "starter questions" at the end of the story. Remember to encourage the student to answer in complete sentences. Then ask the student, "What is the one thing you remember from the story?" Write his answer down and read it back to him.*

The Crow and the Pitcher

A large black crow flew over a long stretch of parched land. He grew thirstier and thirstier! At the edge of a village, he spied a large, deep pitcher at the edge of a patio. He flew down for a drink. To his dismay, there was so little water in the bottom of the pitcher that he could not reach it with his beak.

"I'll push the pitcher over and drink what spills," he thought. But the pitcher was too heavy.

"I'll stretch until I can reach the bottom of the pitcher," he said. But his neck was too short.

"I am too tired to try again," he sighed. So he hopped over into the shade of a tree to think about what else could be done.

As he rested in the cool shade, he noticed a number of large pebbles around the edge of the patio. "I know!" he said to himself. "I can pick up these pebbles one at a time and drop them into the pitcher. As they sink to the bottom, the water will rise above them. Maybe I can collect enough pebbles to make the water rise so that I can reach it."

So he collected the pebbles, one by one, and dropped them into the pitcher. Slowly, pebble by pebble, the water rose. And finally the thirsty crow plunged his beak into the water. He drank and drank until he was full. Refreshed, he spread his wings and flew away.

Moral: Many hard things can be accomplished with patience and perseverance.

Instructor: Why did the crow fly down to the pitcher?
Student: *He was thirsty.*

Instructor: Why couldn't he take a drink?
Student: *His beak couldn't reach the water.*

Instructor: What did he try to do first?
Student: *He tried to push the pitcher over.*

Instructor: Why didn't that work?
Student: *It was too heavy.*

Instructor: What was the second thing the crow tried to do?
Student: *He tried to stretch his neck down to the water.*

Instructor: Did this work?
Student: *No, his neck was too short!*

Instructor: Where did the tired crow go after that?
Student: *He went to rest and think under a tree.*

Instructor: What did he decide to do?
Student: *He decided to drop pebbles into the pitcher.*

Instructor: What happened to the water when the pebbles were dropped in?
Student: *It rose high enough so he could drink it.*

Instructor: What is the moral of the story?
Student: *If you keep trying, you can do many hard things.*

•••••••••••••••••••• **LESSON 63** ••••••••••••••••••••

Days of the week
Months of the year

Instructor: Do you remember the names of the days of the week? Let me read you the poem you memorized about the days of the week. Then, I'd like you to say it back to me.

Note to Instructor: *Read the following poem, and then ask the student to repeat it.*

Days of the Week
Mother Goose rhyme, adapted by Sara Buffington

Monday's child is fair of face,
Tuesday's child is full of grace;
Wednesday's child is ever so sweet,
Thursday's child is tidy and neat;
Friday's child is prone to a giggle,
Saturday's child is easy to tickle;
But the child that is born on restful Sunday
Is happy and cheerful, and loves to play.

Instructor: Good! Now let's say the days of the week together.

TOGETHER: Sunday, Monday, Tuesday, Wednesday, Thursday, Friday, Saturday.

Instructor: Can you count them? How many days are in a week?
Student: *Seven.*

Instructor: A week is made up of seven days. Months are made up of 30 days or 31 days—and one month only has 28 days. Do you remember which month has 28 days?
Student: *February.*

Instructor: I will read you the poem about the months. Then, I'd like you to say it back to me.

The Months
Anonymous

Thirty days hath September,
April, June, and November;
All the rest have thirty-one,
Except for February alone,
Which has four and twenty-four
Till leap year gives it one day more.

Instructor: Let's say the first three months together, three times. Remember, those months are January, February, March.

TOGETHER (three times): January, February, March.

Instructor: Now let's do the next three: April, May, June.

TOGETHER (three times): April, May, June.

Instructor: Now the next three: July, August, September.

TOGETHER (three times): July, August, September.

Instructor: And now the last three: October, November, December.

TOGETHER (three times): October, November, December.

•••••••••••••••••••••   **LESSON 64**   •••••••••••••••••••••

Introducing seasons (Winter)
Copywork: "Winter"
Oral usage: "It was I"

Note to Instructor: *The instructor will need a calendar, a pencil, and paper. The student will need a pencil and paper as well as construction paper and coloring supplies for the enrichment activity.*

Instructor: The winter months are December, January, and February. Say the names of the winter months.

Student: *December, January, February.*

Instructor: "Winter" is the name of a season. We capitalize the names of the months, but we do not capitalize the names of the seasons.

Note to Instructor: *If your family celebrates any holidays in these three winter months, talk to the student about them. Find the dates on the calendar.*

Instructor: How many days does December have?

Note to Instructor: *Help the student go through the poem "The Months" to find the answer.*

Student: *Thirty-one days.*

Instructor: How many days does January have?
Student: *Thirty-one days.*

Instructor: How many days does February have?
Student: *Twenty-eight.*

Instructor: How many days does it have in Leap Year—every four years?
Student: *Twenty-nine.*

Copywork

Help the student write "Winter" as the title on a sheet of paper. Write the names of these three winter months for the student to copy onto his paper. Then have the student draw or cut out a winter picture or pictures showing the season or a holiday celebrated in these months. If the student asks why you are capitalizing "Winter," explain that titles are always capitalized (this rule will be covered later).

Oral Usage Exercise

Note to Instructor: *The subject pronouns "I," "he," and "she" should always be used in the sentence pattern, "It is..." or "This is...." The student should never say, "It is me!" or "It is him!" Read the following dialogue with the student, encouraging him to use the pronouns "I," "he," and "she."*

This lesson also reviews the following usage rules: "See" is the present tense of "to see." "Saw" is the past tense. "Seen" is also a past form of "to see," but must always be used with the helping verb "has" or "have."

Instructor: Who was that in the snow? Begin your answer with, "It was..."
Student: *It was I.*

Instructor: Who threw the snowball? Was it the boy over there? Begin your answer with, "It was..."
Student: *It was he.*

Instructor: Have you seen snow before? Begin your answer with "I..."
Student: *I have seen snow before.*

  Note to Instructor: *If the student uses "seen" alone, remind him to use "have" along with it.*

Instructor: When did you see snow before? Begin your answer with "I..."
Student: *I saw snow last winter.*

  Note to Instructor: *If the student uses "seen," remind him that "seen" cannot be used without the word "have," but that "saw" can be used alone.*

Enrichment Activity

You may collect the student's writings and drawings about the seasons and make a booklet titled, "The Seasons." Today, ask the student to write the words "The Seasons" on the front cover and decorate it. Save the booklet until all four seasons are studied (Lessons 64, 67, 69, and 70).

••••••••••••••••••••• **LESSON 65** •••••••••••••••••••

Introducing abbreviations

Instructor: Can you hear the word "brief" in the middle of "abbreviations"? "Brief" means short. Today we will have a short lesson. Right now the lesson is over!

•••••••••••••••••••   **LESSON 66**   •••••••••••••••••••

Initials
Abbreviations
Copywork: "Winter abbreviations"

Note to Instructor: *The student will need a pencil and paper for this lesson.*

Instructor: We learned that the first letter of a word is its initial letter. The word "initial" means "first" or "beginning." When you write an initial for a word, instead of writing the whole word, you are abbreviating the word. You are writing it in a brief form. Write your full name for me. Now let's look at the first letters of each word. If you abbreviate this name by writing your initials, what would your initials be?

Student: *My initials are __ __ __.*

Instructor: Remember, initials are always capital letters. Initials should always be followed by a period. When we write the names of the months, we often abbreviate them. But we don't use their initials. We use the first three letters of each month's name, and then place a period after those letters. What are the first three letters of December?

Student: *Dec.*

Note to Instructor: *Write these letters out while the student watches. Place a period after the abbreviation. Follow this procedure for January and February as well.*

Instructor: What are the first three letters of January?
Student: *Jan.*

Instructor: What are the first three letters of February?
Student: *Feb.*

Copywork

Ask the student to copy the abbreviations for December, January, and February. Remind him to put a period after each abbreviation.

•   LESSON 67   •

Seasons (Spring)
Noun review
Copywork: "Spring"

Note to Instructor: *Both the instructor and the student will need a pencil and paper. The student will also need seed catalogs for the enrichment activity.*

Instructor: Let's say the definition of a noun together.

TOGETHER: **A noun is the name of a person, place, thing, or idea.**

Instructor: Give me the name of a person. Either a common noun or a proper noun is fine!
Student: *[common noun or proper noun]*

Instructor: Give me the name of a place. Either a common noun or a proper noun is fine!
Student: *[common noun or proper noun]*

Instructor: Name a thing in this room for me.
Student: *[chair, spoon]*

Instructor: Now, can you think of the name of an idea? Remember, an idea is something you think about in your mind, but cannot see or touch.
Student: *[idea]*

Note to Instructor: *If necessary, prompt the student for feelings such as love, fear, anger, happiness, or for a character quality such as patience, persistence, or obedience.*

Instructor: We have talked about December, January, and February—the winter months. Do you know what season comes after winter? Spring comes after winter! The spring months are March, April, and May. Repeat those after me.
Student: *March, April, May.*

Instructor: What are the first three letters of March?
Student: *Mar.*

Note to Instructor: *Write these letters out while the student watches. Place a period after the abbreviation. Follow this procedure for April as well.*

Instructor: What are the first three letters of April?

Student: *Apr.*

Instructor: What are the first three letters of May?

Student: *May!*

Instructor: May is only three letters long, so we don't need an abbreviation for it! Remember, abbreviations of months are always capitalized and have a period after them. The names of months are always capitalized when they are written in full, because they are proper names. But "winter" and "spring" are seasons. Their names are not capitalized.

Copywork

Help the student write "Spring" as the title on a sheet of paper. Write the names of these three spring months for the student to copy onto his paper. Then ask the student to draw or cut out a spring picture or pictures showing the season or a holiday celebrated in these months.

Enrichment Activity

You may plan to collect the student's writing and drawing about the seasons and make a booklet titled "The Seasons." For "Spring," the student may use seed catalogs to cut out pictures of spring blooming plants, bulbs, and trees. He may wish to label the pictures to identify the names of the flowers.

····················· **LESSON 68** ·····················

Action verbs
Oral usage: "Was/Were"

Note to Instructor: *The student will need a pencil and paper for the enrichment activity.*

Instructor: **A verb is a word that does an action, shows a state of being, links two words to-gether, or helps another verb.** Let's repeat the first part of that definition three times.

TOGETHER (three times): **A verb is a word that does an action.**

Instructor: Now I want you to repeat the second part of the definition one time: **Shows a state of being.** Repeat that for me.

Student: *Shows a state of being.*

Instructor: **Links two words together.**

Student: *Links two words together.*

Instructor: **Or helps another verb.**

Student: *Or helps another verb.*

Instructor: Now, let's see if we can find some action verbs in the story "The Crow and the Pitcher."

Note to Instructor: *Go back to Lesson 62, "The Crow and the Pitcher," and read it aloud to the student. Help the student to follow along with your finger or a marker. After you and the student read each sentence aloud, stop and help him to find the action verbs. In order of appearance, they are: flew, grew, spied, flew, reach, push, drinks, spill, thought, stretch, reach, said, try, sighed, hopped, think, rested, noticed, know, said, pick, drop, sink, rise, collect, make, rise, reach, collected, dropped, rose, plunged, drank, drank, spread, flew. Use your discretion: You do not need to read the whole story if his attention span is short.*

Oral Usage Exercise

Note to Instructor: *Use "was" when speaking of one; use "were" when speaking of more than one or when speaking of "you."*

Instructor: I am going to read some sentences to you. I want you to tell me which word goes in the blank: "was" or "were?" If the sentence speaks of only one person, choose "was." If it speaks of more than one, use "were." Also use "were" along with the word "you."

Instructor: Brenda and Frank _____ playing store.

Student: *Brenda and Frank were playing store.*

Instructor: Carl and Holly_____ in a spelling contest.
Student: *Carl and Holly were in a spelling contest.*

Instructor: Daisy _____ in the swimming pool.
Student: *Daisy was in the swimming pool.*

Instructor: You _____at home yesterday.
Student: *You were at home yesterday.*

Instructor: Remember, use "were" with the word "you"! The children_____ having a picnic.
Student: *The children were having a picnic.*

Instructor: The mother _____ enjoying the good weather.
Student: *The mother was enjoying the good weather.*

Instructor: The boy and the girl _____ playing soccer.
Student: *The boy and the girl were playing soccer.*

Enrichment Activity

If the student is writing easily, he may make a list of the verbs in "The Crow and the Pitcher." Title his list "The Crow's Action Verbs."

• • • • • • • • • • • • • • • • • • •   **LESSON 69**   • • • • • • • • • • • • • • • • • •

Pronouns
Seasons (Summer)
Copywork: "Summer"

Note to Instructor: *The instructor will need a pencil, paper, and a calendar. The student will need a pencil, paper, drawing supplies, and magazines for summer pictures.*

Read the student the following list of pronouns three times. If the student can chime in with any of the pronouns, encourage him to do so, but he does not need to memorize the list.

I, me, my, mine;
you, your, yours;
he, she, him, her, it, his, hers, its;
we, us, our, ours;
they, them, their, theirs.

Instructor: What two seasons have we learned about?
Student: *We have learned about winter and spring.*

Instructor: The winter months are December, January and February. Repeat those months for me.
Student: *December, January, February.*

Instructor: The spring months are March, April, and May. Repeat those months for me.
Student: *March, April, May.*

Instructor: The summer months are June, July, August. Say the names of these summer months with me.

TOGETHER: June, July, August.

Instructor: Can you tell me the abbreviations for June and July? Remember, use the first three letters of the month.

  Note to Instructor: *Write the abbreviations as the student says them. Point out the period after the abbreviation.*

Student: *Jun., Jul.*

Instructor: What are the first three letters of August?
Student: *Aug.*

Instructor: Remember, summer is the name of a season. So we do not capitalize the word "summer."

Note to Instructor: *If your family celebrates any holidays in these summer months, talk to the student about them. Find the dates on the calendar.*

Copywork

Help the student write "Summer" as the title on a sheet of paper. Write the names of these three summer months for the student to copy onto his paper. Then have the student draw or cut out a summer picture or pictures showing the season, or a holiday celebrated in these months.

Enrichment Activity

Ask the student to continue illustrating "Summer" with pictures and cutouts for his "Seasons" booklet.

·   **LESSON 70**   ·

Seasons (Fall)
Copywork: "Fall"
Poem review: "The Months" (Lesson 43)

Note to Instructor: *The instructor will need a pencil, paper, and a calendar. The student will need a pencil and paper as well as drawing supplies and magazines.*

Review "The Months" today.

Instructor: What three seasons have we learned?

Student: *We have learned winter, spring, summer.*

Instructor: I am going to say those months for you. Then we will try to say them together three times. December, January, February, March, April, May, June, July, August.

Together (three times): December, January, February, March, April, May, June, July, August.

Instructor: We have one more season to learn about! The fall months are September, October, and November. Say the names of the fall months with me three times.

Together (three times): September, October, November.

Instructor: Sometimes the season "fall" is also called "autumn." Remember, "fall" and "autumn" are seasons, so we don't capitalize them.

Note to Instructor: *If your family celebrates any holidays in these three fall months, talk to the student about them. Find the dates on the calendar.*

Instructor: Now let's write out the abbreviations for September, October, and November. You tell me the first three letters of each word, and I will write them out. I will capitalize each abbreviation and put a period at the end of each one. What are the abbreviations for these months?

Student: *Sep., Oct., Nov.*

Instructor: Sometimes you will also see September abbreviated as "Sept."

Copywork ──

Help the student write "Fall" as the title on a sheet of paper. Write the names of these three fall months for the student to copy. Then have the student draw or cut out a fall picture or pictures showing the season or a holiday celebrated in these months.

Enrichment Activity

Continue to work on the fall section of the student's booklet, "The Seasons."

• **LESSON 71** • • • • • • • • • • • • • • • • • •

Seasons
Holidays

Note to Instructor: *Both the instructor and the student will need a pencil and paper.*

Instructor: Let's try to say the names of all the months together. I'll say them first, and then we'll say them together twice. January, February, March, April, May, June, July, August, September, October, November, December.

TOGETHER (twice): January, February, March, April, May, June, July, August, September, October, November, December.

Instructor: The seasons are winter, spring, summer, and fall. Repeat those for me.

Student: *Winter, spring, summer, fall.*

Instructor: When we were talking and writing about the seasons, you drew or cut out pictures about what happens in those months. Most seasons have holidays that families celebrate. When we write, the names of holidays are capitalized. We are going to talk about holidays that we celebrate. I am going to write the name of the holiday, using capital letters. You will copy three of these holidays.

Note to Instructor: *Talk with the student about holidays you celebrate. Write the names of the holidays for the student to copy. Point out that you are beginning the special, proper names of these holidays with capital letters.*

Copywork

Depending on his writing ability, have the student copy the names of three, four, or five holidays your family celebrates.

Enrichment Activity

Help the student to write the days of the week from memory.

······ **LESSON 72** ······

Pronouns (Capitalization of "I")
Copywork: "Using 'I'"
Oral usage: "Sit/Set"

Note to Instructor: *Both the instructor and the student will need a pencil and paper.*

Instructor: Do you remember when we pretended that you were knocking on the door, and I asked, "Who is it?" Let's pretend that again. Go over and knock on the door. "Who is it?" Do you remember the proper answer?

Student: *It is I.*

Instructor: "I" refers to you! "I" is a pronoun because it stands for a noun—your name! Whenever you use the pronoun "I," it is always capitalized. I will write this sentence out for you, and then I will ask you to copy it.

Note to Instructor: *Write "It is I" on a piece of paper. Show the student the capital "I." Then, ask the student to copy the sentence with proper spacing and capitalization. Remind him to end the sentence with a period.*

Instructor: Whenever you are referring to yourself and another person, always use the other person's name first. Let's pretend that you and I are both knocking on the door, and that someone else calls, "Who is it?" You should answer by putting my name before "I." Answer the question "Who is it?" for both of us, beginning your sentence with "It is…"

Student: *It is [instructor's name] and I.*

Instructor: I will write that out for you.

Note to Instructor: *Write the sentence for the student, pointing out the capital "I."*

Copywork

Choose one of the following sentences, depending on the student's ability.

It is I.

Emma and I ate lunch.

I have three friends named me, myself, and I.

Oral Usage Exercise

Note to Instructor: *Use "set" if you are referring to putting or placing an object. Use "sit" if you mean "to sit down" or "to rest."*

Instructor:	"Sit" and "set" mean two different things. If you need to sit down or rest, use the word "sit." If you have an object that you are putting down or placing somewhere else, use "set." I will read you some sentences. Repeat them back to me by placing "sit" or "set" in the blank.

Instructor: You are tired. Please ___ down.
Student: *You are tired. Please sit down.*

Instructor: Elizabeth, will you ___the groceries on the table?
Student: *Elizabeth, will you set the groceries on the table?*

Instructor: Go in the bedroom and ____down.
Student: *Go in the bedroom and sit down.*

Instructor: I was ____on my chair, thinking.
Student: *I was sitting on my chair, thinking.*

Instructor: Grandmother, please _____ the teakettle on the stove.
Student: *Grandmother, please set the teakettle on the stove.*

Instructor: Be quiet and ____down, right now!
Student: *Be quiet and sit down, right now!*

LESSON 73 •••••••••••••••••••••

Oral composition: "A Story about Me"

Note to Instructor: *Both the instructor and the student will need a pencil and paper for this lesson. The student may need drawing supplies for the enrichment activity.*

Have the student tell a story about himself. Give him these "story openers" and ask him what happens next. This story can be four sentences long—or as long as you wish! Have the student act out the action verbs of his story when he gets to them. As the student tells the story, write down his sentences. When he is finished, show him all of the capitalized "I" pronouns. Then, ask him to copy out one or more of the sentences that you have written. Remind the student that "I" is always capitalized.

Story starters (choose one if the student needs help beginning his story):

- "One day I took my favorite stuffed animals outside for tea."
- "I was walking along the road—and I stepped in quicksand!"
- "It was the day before my birthday. When I came into my brother's room, he hid something quickly!"
- "I discovered a baby kitten on the sidewalk in front of my house."
- "One morning, I woke up and discovered I had turned into a raptor."
- "One morning, I woke up and discovered I had turned into a bunny."

Enrichment Activity

Ask the student to illustrate his story or to write a sequel.

••••••••••••••••••• **LESSON 74** •••••••••••••••••••

Story-poem narration: "The Three Little Kittens"

Note to Instructor: *Read the following poem aloud to the student, and then ask the "starter questions" at the end of the poem. Remember to encourage the student to answer in complete sentences. Then ask the student, "What is the one thing you remember from the poem?" Write his answer down and read it back to him.*

The Three Little Kittens
Traditional

Three little kittens, they lost their mittens,
And they began to cry.
"Oh, Mommy dear,
We sadly fear,
Our mittens we have lost!"
"What! Lost your mittens,
You naughty kittens,
Then you shall have no pie!"
"Meow, meow, meow, meow,
We shall have no pie."

The three little kittens, they found their mittens,
And they began to cry.
"Oh, Mommy dear,
See here, see here,
Our mittens we have found."
"What! Found your mittens,
You good little kittens,
Then you shall have some pie."
"Purr, purr, purr, purr,
Yes, we shall have some pie!"

The three little kittens put on their mittens,
And soon ate up the pie;
"Oh, Mommy dear,
We greatly fear,
Our mittens we have soiled."

"What! Soiled your mittens,
You naughty kittens!"
Then they began to sigh,
"Meow, meow, meow, meow."
Oh, they began to sigh.

The three little kittens, they washed their mittens,
And hung them up to dry;
"Oh, Mommy dear,
Look here, look here,
Our mittens we have washed."
"What! Washed your mittens,
You darling kittens!
But I smell a rat close by!
Hush! Hush! Hush! Hush!
Yes, I smell a rat close by!"

Instructor: How many kittens were there?
Student: *There were three kittens.*

Instructor: What did the kittens lose?
Student: *They lost their mittens.*

Instructor: How did their mother react when she heard the kittens lost their mittens?
Student: *She was angry and she said they could not have pie.*

Instructor: Why did the mother change her mind and let the kittens eat pie?
Student: *The kittens found their mittens.*

Instructor: Because they ate the pie with their mittens on, what happened to the mittens?
Student: *They got dirty.*

Instructor: How did their mother react when she heard the mittens were dirty?
Student: *She told them that they were naughty.*

Instructor: Then what did the kittens do to their dirty mittens?
Student: *They washed them.*

Instructor: How did their mother react when she heard the kittens had washed their mittens?
Student: *She was happy with the kittens.*

Instructor: What do you think will happen to the rat after the story ends?
Student: *The mother might catch the rat!*

Note to Instructor: *Remember to write down the student's summary of the story. Let him look back over your written version of his narration after you have finished.*

• • • • • • • • • • • • • • • •   LESSON 75   • • • • • • • • • • • • • • • •

Nouns, verbs, and pronouns in "The Three Little Kittens"
Copywork: "The Kittens"
Poem review: "The Months" (Lesson 43)

Note to Instructor: *The student will need a pencil and paper.*

Review "The Months" today.

Instructor: Let's say the definition of a **noun** together.

TOGETHER: **A noun is the name of a person, place, thing, or idea.**

Instructor: Names of animals are also nouns. Let's find the nouns in the first part of "The Three Little Kittens."

Note to Instructor: *Read the first stanza to the student while you help him to follow along. He should identify the nouns "kittens," "mittens," "mommy," and "pie."*

Instructor: Is the noun "kittens" a common noun or a proper noun?
Student: *The noun "kittens" is a common noun.*

Note to Instructor: *If necessary, remind the student that a proper noun would refer to one particular kitten.*

Instructor: How many kittens were there?
Student: *There were three kittens.*

Instructor: Can you give each kitten a proper name?

Note to Instructor: *Help the student find a proper name for each kitten.*

Instructor: In the first line of the poem, the kittens did something active. What did they do?
Student: *They lost their mittens.*

Instructor: "Lost" is an action verb. Remember: **A verb is a word that does an action.** What action do the kittens do in the second line?
Student: *The kittens cry.*

Instructor: In the last verse of the poem, what did the kittens do with their mittens?
Student: *The kittens washed their mittens.*

Instructor: "Washed" is an action verb. In the first line of the last stanza, can you find a pronoun that refers to the kittens? Who washed the mittens?

Student: *They washed their mittens.*

Instructor: It is easier to say, "They washed their mittens" than "The kittens washed the kittens' mittens!" When the mother says that she smells a rat, what word does she use to refer to herself?

Student: *She calls herself "I."*

Instructor: The pronoun "I" is capitalized. If the kittens have to wear mittens to eat their pie, what season is it—spring, summer, fall, or winter?

Student: *It must be winter!*

Instructor: Yes, because it is cold outside! What months are in the winter season?

Student: *December, January, February.*

Copywork

Ask the student to copy one of the following sentences:

They began to cry.

Hush. I smell a rat close by.

The three little kittens put on their mittens.

········· **LESSON 76** ··············

Initials
Months of the year
Days of the week
Pronouns
Copywork: "Days of the Week"

Note to Instructor: *Both the instructor and the student will need a pencil and paper.*

Instructor: Let's review some lessons that we've already learned. The first letter of a name is the initial letter. Let's write out the initials of people that we know. Remember, initials are capitalized and have periods after them.

Note to Instructor: *Supply the student with three names of family members or other people he knows well. Write out the full names. Then ask the student to write the initials for each full name.*

Instructor: The period that follows an initial is called a punctuation mark. Remember, periods also follow the abbreviations for the months. Let's say the names of the months together.

TOGETHER: January, February, March, April, May, June, July, August, September, October, November, December.

Instructor: Now say the days of the week with me, beginning with Sunday.

TOGETHER: Sunday, Monday, Tuesday, Wednesday, Thursday, Friday, Saturday.

Instructor: We've already reviewed the definitions of nouns and verbs. Now, let's review the definition of a pronoun. **A pronoun is a word that takes the place of a noun.** Let's say that together twice.

TOGETHER (twice): **A pronoun is a word that takes the place of a noun.**

Instructor: I will read the list of pronouns. Say as many of the pronouns as you can along with me.

I, me, my, mine;
you, your, yours;
he, she, him, her, it, his, hers, its;
we, us, our, ours;
they, them, their, theirs.

Instructor: Now, I will read you some sentences. Can you fill in the blank with a pronoun? On Monday, Jane rode on a bus. _____ went to visit Dad at work.

Student:	*She went to visit Dad at work.*

Instructor: On Tuesday, Dad stayed home from work. _____ took Jane to the zoo.

Student: *He took Jane to the zoo.*

Instructor: On Wednesday, Jane went back to the zoo to see the tiger. The zoo was her favorite place. She loved _____.

Student: *She loved it.*

Instructor: On Thursday, Jane and Mommy bought the tiger for a house pet. _____ both love tigers.

Student: *They both love tigers.*

Instructor: On Friday, Jane, Mommy, and Daddy decided the tiger would like to have an adventure. So they went on a boat ride and took the tiger with _____.

Student: *So they went on a boat ride and took the tiger with them.*

Instructor: On Saturday, Jane and Mommy and Daddy fed the tiger everything in the refrigerator and in the freezer. The tiger was still hungry. ____ wanted more.

Student: *It [or he, or she] wanted more.*

Instructor: On Sunday, Jane and Mommy and Daddy took the tiger back to the zoo. The zookeeper said, "Only a silly family would want a tiger for a pet! _____ must be a silly family!"

Student: *You must be a silly family.*

Copywork

Write out the days of the week for the student. Ask him to copy as many as he is able.

Enrichment Activity

Ask the student to write the days of week in order from memory.

·   **LESSON 77**   · · · · · · · · · · · · · · · · · · ·

Abbreviations (Addresses)

Note to Instructor: *Both the instructor and the student will need a pencil and paper for the lesson.*

Instructor: Can you tell me your address?

Note to Instructor: *If necessary, prompt student to give the full address.*

Instructor: Today we are going to learn how to abbreviate your address. An abbreviation is a short-ened form of a word. It usually ends with a period. Today I am going to show you how to write the abbreviations for "Street," "Avenue," and "Road."

Note to Instructor: *As you explain the abbreviations, write them out for the student to see. Point out the capital letters and periods. You may also explain any other abbreviations in the student's address.*

Instructor: We abbreviate the word "Street" as St. We abbreviate the word "Avenue" as Ave. We ab-breviate the word "Road" as Rd. Now let's write out your address, using the proper abbre-viations.

Note to Instructor: *Write out the student's street address for him to copy. Be sure to use the address abbre-viations. Do not write out the city, state, and ZIP code yet. Ask the student to copy his street address with the proper abbreviations.*

Instructor: The post office has special abbreviations for the names of states. They do not have peri-ods like regular abbreviations. Every state abbreviation has two letters, and both letters are capitalized. The abbreviation for our state is _____.

Note to Instructor: *Using the current U.S. Post Office abbreviations, write out the student's city, state, and ZIP code. Ask the student to copy this line under the first address line.*

Instructor: Now you know how to write your address with abbreviations.

Note to Instructor: *Write out the names and addresses of family members or friends. Point out abbrevia-tions and state abbreviations to the student as you write.*

· **LESSON 78** · · · · · · · · · · · · · · · · · · ·

Introducing titles of respect
Copywork: "Titles of respect"

Note to Instructor: *Both the instructor and the student will need a pencil and paper.*

Instructor: Have you noticed that sometimes people's names start with Mr. or Mrs. or Dr. or Miss? These are called "titles of respect." They show that we respect the position of that person. When these titles are written, they are often abbreviated. Do you remember that an abbreviation is brief—meaning "short"? I am going to show you the abbreviated (short) way to write some common titles of respect.

Note to Instructor: *Write out the following titles of respect with their abbreviations. Point out the capital letters and periods as you do so.*

Mister	Mr.	This is a title for a man.
Mistress	Mrs.	This is a title for a married woman.
Doctor	Dr.	This is a title for a physician or for someone with a special degree from a university.
Miss	—	This is not an abbreviation, but a title of courtesy for an unmarried girl or woman.
*	Ms.	*Ms. is an abbreviation for either Mistress or Miss. You should use it when you do not know whether a woman would prefer to be called Mrs. or Miss.

Note to Instructor: *Run your finger under the words as you read the following sentences aloud. Ask the student to follow along:*

Mr. Smith likes to garden.

Mrs. Smith is a writer.

Dr. Rosenberg works at the hospital.

Ms. Lopez is a nurse.

Miss Collins teaches art.

Instructor: Mr., Mrs., Dr., Ms., and Miss are always written with a capital letter.

Copywork

Have the student copy as many of the following sentences as seems appropriate.

Mr. stands for Mister.

Dr. stands for Doctor.

Mrs. refers to a married woman.

Miss refers to an unmarried woman.

Ms. can refer to any woman.

Enrichment Activity

Have the student write several sentences that tell what family members and friends do for a living. Make sure that the student uses the appropriate titles in each sentence.

•••••••••••••••••••••   **LESSON 79**   •••••••••••••••••••••

Titles of respect
Poem review: "The Caterpillar" (Lesson 2)

Note to Instructor: *The student will need a pencil and paper.*

Review "The Caterpillar" today.

Instructor: What mark of punctuation follows each abbreviation?
Student: *A period.*

Instructor: Which title of respect is not an abbreviation?
Student: *Miss.*

Instructor: Which abbreviation stands for a married woman?
Student: *Mrs.*

Instructor: What is the abbreviation for Doctor?
Student: *Dr.*

Instructor: What title should you use if you don't know whether a woman would like to be called Mrs. or Miss?
Student: *Ms.*

Note to Instructor: *I would not introduce the abbreviation Jr. or Sr. now unless the student notices that a close family member uses it.*

Instructor: I am going to say each title of respect. On your paper, write the proper abbreviation for each one.

Note to Instructor: *If the student begins to write a title incorrectly, stop him and show him the correct form of the title.*

Instructor: Write abbreviations for the following titles of respect: Mister, Miss, Mistress, Ms., Doctor.

LESSON 80 •••••••••••••••••••

Cumulative poem review

Instructor: Today we are going to review all of the poems you have worked on so far. When we recite a poem, we begin with the title and author. I will read each poem to you, and then I want you to try to say the poem back to me. Remember: Stand up straight! Don't fidget while you're reciting! And speak in a nice, loud, slow voice.

Note to Instructor: *Read each poem to the student before asking him to repeat it. If he repeats it accurately, move on to the next poem. If he stumbles, ask him to repeat the line he cannot remember three times, and make a note to review that poem daily until it is mastered. Remind the student that "Anonymous" means that we do not know who wrote the poem.*

Lesson	Poem	Author
2	"The Caterpillar"	Christina G. Rossetti
15	"Work"	Anonymous
27	"Hearts Are Like Doors"	Anonymous
35	"Days of the Week"	Mother Goose rhyme, adapted by Sara Buffington
43	"The Months"	Mother Goose rhyme

•••••••••••••••••••• **LESSON 81** ••••••••••••••••••••

Poem memorization: "Mr. Nobody"

Note to Instructor: *For this lesson, read the whole poem aloud. Ask the student: Who do you think Mr. Nobody is?*

Mr. Nobody
Anonymous

I know a funny little man,
    As quiet as a mouse,
Who does the mischief that is done
    In everybody's house!
There's no one ever sees his face,
    And yet we all agree
That every plate we break was cracked
    By Mr. Nobody.

'Tis he who always tears our books,
    Who leaves the door ajar,
He pulls the buttons from our shirts,
    And scatters pins afar;
That squeaking door will always squeak,
    For, prithee, don't you see,
We leave the oiling to be done
    By Mr. Nobody.

The finger marks upon the door
    By none of us are made;
We never leave the blinds unclosed,
    To let the curtains fade.
The ink we never spill; the boots
    That lying 'round you see
Are not our boots—they all belong
    To Mr. Nobody.

Note to Instructor: *Read the first stanza to the student three times in a row. Encourage the student to chime in with you as he becomes more familiar with the words.*

······· **LESSON 82** ·······

Capitalization in poetry
Copywork: "Mr. Nobody"
Poem practice: Stanza one of "Mr. Nobody" (Lesson 81)

Note to Instructor: *The student will need a pencil and paper for this activity as well as drawing supplies for the enrichment activity.*

Read all of "Mr. Nobody" to the student. Then read stanza one three times in a row. Encourage the student to begin to say the lines along with you.

Instructor: What is the name of this poem?

Student: *The name of the poem is "Mr. Nobody"*

Instructor: The name of the poem is its title. All important words in a poem title should be capitalized. The first word of the title and every other word which is not a little word, like "and" or "the" or "of," should begin with a capital letter. Let's look at the titles of your other poems.

The Caterpillar

Work

Hearts Are Like Doors

Days of the Week

The Months

Instructor: The first word of every title is capitalized. So are all the other words except for "of" and "the." Look at the poem "Mr. Nobody" again. The first word in every line begins with a capital letter. Let's look down the first words and name the capital letters together.

Note to Instructor: *Move your finger down the left-hand margin of the page next to "Mr. Nobody" and help the student identify the capital letters.*

Instructor: Titles of poems and the first word of every line should be capitalized.

Copywork

Choose one of the following options: Ask the student to copy from "Mr. Nobody":
1. The title and the first line of the first stanza
2. The title and the first two lines of the first stanza
3. The title, the "Anonymous" author attribution, and the first four lines of the first stanza.

Remind the student that "Mr." is an abbreviation for "Mister." It should have both a capital letter and a period.

Enrichment Activity

Invite the student to illustrate one or more stanzas of "Mr. Nobody."

••••••••••••••••••••• LESSON 83 ••••••••••••••••••••

Pronouns
Oral usage: "Is/Are"
Poem practice: Stanza one of "Mr. Nobody" (Lesson 81)

Note to Instructor: *Continue work on stanza one of "Mr. Nobody."*

Review helpful poetry memorization techniques from Lesson 2.

Instructor: Let's say the definition of a **pronoun** together.

TOGETHER: **A pronoun is a word that takes the place of a noun.**

Instructor: I will read the list of pronouns. Say as many of the pronouns as you can along with me.

> I, me, my, mine;
> you, your, yours;
> he, she, him, her, it, his, hers, its;
> we, us, our, ours;
> they, them, their, theirs.

Today we are going to talk about "we, us, our, ours." I am going to read some sentences and then ask you a question. I want you to answer using one of the pronouns "we, us, our, ours."

Instructor: We planted sunflower seeds. Who planted sunflower seeds?
Student: *We planted sunflower seeds.*

Instructor: For whom did the seeds grow?
Student: *The seeds grew for us.*

Instructor: Now, who owns the flowers?
Student: *Now, the flowers are ours.*

Instructor: Are they your flowers?
Student: *They are our flowers.*

Oral Usage Exercise ————————————————————

Instructor: If you are speaking about one person or thing, use the word "is." If you are speaking about more than one person or thing, use the word "are." I will read you several sentences. Choose the correct word to put in the blank.

Instructor: My pencil ___in my pocket.
Student: *My pencil is in my pocket.*

Instructor: My pencils ___all yellow.
Student: *My pencils are all yellow.*

Instructor: Cherries ____my favorite fruit.
Student: *Cherries are my favorite fruit.*

Instructor: I like cherries because they___ red.
Student: *I like cherries because they are red.*

Instructor: Mr. Nance and Dr. Alvarez _____ going fishing together.
Student: *Mr. Nance and Dr. Alvarez are going fishing together.*

· · · · · · · · · · · · · · · · · · ·   **LESSON 84**   · · · · · · · · · · · · · · · · · ·

Oral composition: "Mr. Nobody at Our House"
Copywork: "Mr. Nobody at Our House"
Poem practice: "Mr. Nobody" (Lesson 81)

Note to Instructor: *Both the instructor and the student will need a pencil and paper.*

Read stanza one of "Mr. Nobody" to the student. Ask the student to recite these lines back to you. Then read stanza two out loud to the student three times in a row. Ask the student to join in whenever he is able.

Instructor: Can you tell me some of the things in our house that are done by Mr. Nobody?

Note to Instructor: *Encourage the student to think about the messes that no one admits to! Help him to form these ideas into complete sentences. Write them down in neat handwriting and help him to read the sentences out loud. Write "Mr. Nobody at Our House" at the top of the paper.*

Instructor: The title of our own composition is "Mr. Nobody at Our House." Which words are capitalized? Which word is not capitalized?

Copywork

Ask the student to copy one of the sentences you composed for the lesson.

Enrichment Activity

Ask the student to write a description (either a list or a paragraph) about the things that Mr. Nobody does at your house.

· **LESSON 85** · · · · · · · · · · · · · · · · · · ·

Abbreviations
Initials and addresses
Poem practice: Stanzas one and two of "Mr. Nobody" (Lesson 81)

Note to Instructor: *Both the instructor and the student need a pencil and paper. The student also needs one business-size envelope for the lesson.*

Read stanzas one and two of "Mr. Nobody" out loud to the student three times. Then ask the student to begin reciting the poem and to go as far as possible.

Draw light lines on a business-size envelope to guide the student in properly addressing a real envelope. Help the student address the envelope to himself. He should write his name using initials for his first and middle name. Help him to use the correct road, street, lane, or avenue abbreviations for his own address. Also help him use the correct state abbreviation. Remind the student that most abbreviations have a capital letter and a period, but that state abbreviations are special. Both letters of a state abbreviation are capitalized, and there is no punctuation mark. When the envelope is completed, ask the student to mail himself a picture that he has drawn.

••••••••••••••••••••• **LESSON 86** •••••••••••••••••••

Capitalization and punctuation in poetry
Copywork: "The Star"
Poem practice: Stanzas one and two of "Mr. Nobody" (Lesson 81)

Note to Instructor: *The student will need a pencil and paper.*

Read stanzas one and two of "Mr. Nobody" out loud to the student twice. Then ask the student to begin reciting the poem and to go as far as possible. Next, read the final stanza of "Mr. Nobody" out loud to the student three times. Ask the student to try to recite the poem from the beginning.

Later in the day, repeat this process.

Copywork

Read the student the poem "The Star," by Jane Taylor (1783–1824). Ask the student to finish one of the following assignments. Remind him that titles and first words of poem lines should be capitalized.
1. Copy the title, author, and first line.
2. Copy the title, author, and first two lines.
3. Copy the title, author, and first stanza.

The Star
Jane Taylor

Twinkle, twinkle, little star,
How I wonder what you are!
Up above the world so high,
Like a diamond in the sky.

When the blazing sun is gone,
When he nothing shines upon,
Then you show your little light,
Twinkle, twinkle, all the night.

Then the traveller in the dark,
Thanks you for your tiny spark.
He could not see which way to go
If you did not twinkle so.

In the dark blue sky you keep
And often through my curtains peep,
For you never shut your eye
Till the sun is in the sky.

As your bright and tiny spark
Lights the traveller in the dark –
Though I know not what you are,
Twinkle, twinkle, little star.

• • • • • • • • • • • • • • • • • • • **LESSON 87** • • • • • • • • • • • • • • • • • •

Story narration: "The Boy Who Cried Wolf"
Poem practice: "Mr. Nobody" (Lesson 81)

Notes to Instructor: *The instructor will need a pencil and paper.*

Read all three stanzas of "Mr. Nobody" out loud to the student twice. Ask the student to begin reciting and to go as far as possible. For any stanzas that the student cannot remember, repeat them out loud three times.

Read the following Aesop's Fable aloud to the student, and then ask the "starter questions" at the end of the story. Remember to encourage the student to answer in complete sentences. Then ask the student, "What is the one thing you remember from the story?" Write his answer down and read it back to him.

The Boy Who Cried Wolf

A young boy kept sheep on a hillside near his home in a village. They were his very own sheep, and when the sheep were sheared, he was allowed to keep the money from the sale of the wool.

While he was on the hillside one warm spring day, he could see the women working in their gardens, and the men working together repairing the thatched roofs. The young shepherd thought that watching the sheep was boring and so he decided to play a trick on the villagers. He ran down the hillside toward the village loudly screaming, "Wolf! Wolf! There is a wolf after my sheep!"

The villagers quickly stopped their work and ran frantically up the hill to rescue the boy's sheep from the wolves. When they arrived where the boy's sheep were quietly grazing, the boy was waiting there. He laughed at them for hurrying so when there was no wolf.

The boy was so amused by the trick he had played on the villagers that he decided to try it again the next week. He ran down the hillside again, loudly screaming, "Wolf! Wolf!"

The kind villagers again quickly stopped their work and ran frantically up the hill to rescue the boy's sheep from the wolves. When they arrived where the boy's sheep were grazing, the boy laughed at them again for hurrying so when there was not a wolf.

The next week a real wolf attacked his flock and started to kill the little lambs.

The boy ran down the hillside, loudly screaming, "Wolf! Wolf! There is a wolf after my sheep!"

But the villagers thought he was just playing another trick on them. "Leave us alone!" they snapped at him. "We have work to do! Go back up to your sheep and stop annoying us." And they turned their backs on the boy. No one came to help him—and he lost all of his sheep to the hungry wolf.

Moral: If you tell lies, people will not believe you when you do tell the truth.

Instructor: What was the job of the young boy?
Student: *He watched a flock of sheep.*

Instructor: Whom did the sheep belong to?
Student: *They belonged to the boy.*

Instructor: When the boy became bored, what did he decide to do?
Student: *He decided to play a trick on the villagers.*

Instructor: What did he tell the villagers?
Student: *He said a wolf was eating his sheep.*

Instructor: How did the villagers respond to the news?
Student: *They ran up the hill to help him.*

Instructor: What did they discover when they ran up the hill?
Student: *The boy was lying. There was no wolf.*

Instructor: Did the boy feel bad about lying?
Student: *No, he thought it was funny.*

Instructor: Because the boy thought the trick was so funny, what did he do the next week?
Student: *He played the trick again.*

Instructor: What happened the week after that?
Student: *A wolf really did attack his sheep.*

Instructor: When the boy told all the villagers about the real wolf, what did they do?
Student: *They kept working.*

Instructor: Why didn't they help the boy?

Student: *They thought he was playing another trick.*

Instructor: What happened to the boy's sheep?
Student: *They were killed by the wolf.*

Instructor: What is the moral of the story?
Student: *If you tell lies, no one will believe you when you tell the truth.*

•   **LESSON 88**   • • • • • • • • • • • • • • • • • •

Introducing writing dates
Copywork: "Writing dates"
Poem review: "Mr. Nobody" (Lesson 81)

Note to Instructor: *Both the instructor and the student will need a pencil and paper.*

Read all three stanzas of "Mr. Nobody" out loud to the student twice. Ask the student to begin reciting and to go as far as possible. For any stanzas that the student cannot remember, repeat them out loud three times.

Instructor: We have talked about the names of the days of the week. Let's say them together.

TOGETHER: Sunday, Monday, Tuesday, Wednesday, Thursday, Friday, Saturday.

Instructor: We have also talked about the names of the months. Let's say those together as well.

TOGETHER: January, February, March, April, May, June, July, August, September, October, November, December.

Instructor: Every day of the year has a date. A date is made up of the month of the year, a number telling you what day of the month it is, and a number telling you what year it is. For example, "Thirty days hath September." September has thirty days in it. So the last day of September would be September 30. Every day of the month has a number. Today is [today's date]. It is the [number] day of the month of [name of month]. Every year also has a number. This year is 20—. Last year was 20—. Next year will be 20—. You were born in _____.

Note to Instructor: *Write out for the student the date on which he was born, and the dates on which any siblings or friends of a similar age were born.*

Instructor: When we write a date, we write the month and the day. Then we put a comma between the day and the year.

Note to Instructor: *Show student how to make a comma.*

Instructor: I want you to practice making ten neat commas on your own paper.

Copywork

Ask the student to copy one of the following phrases or sentences. Write the assignment out for the student.

[The date on which the student was born, including month, day, and year, with a comma between day and year]

I was born on [date].

I was born on [date] during the [season—winter, spring, summer or fall].

• **LESSON 89** • • • • • • • • • • • • • • • • • •

Dates
Poem review: "Mr. Nobody" (Lesson 81)

Note to Instructor: *Both the instructor and the student will need a pencil and paper for this lesson.*

Continue to review "Mr. Nobody."

Discuss important dates (days, months, and years) for your family with the student: birthdays of parents and grandparents, holidays the family celebrates, national holidays, or dates of religious significance. Write these dates out. Ask the student to copy four, six, or eight of these dates onto his own paper. Remind him to capitalize the names of months and to place commas between the day and year of each date.

You may also use any of the following dates:

March 15, 44 BC	*The Ides of March*	*Julius Caesar was killed*
October 14, 1066	*—*	*The Battle of Hastings*
June 15, 1215	*—*	*King John signed the Magna Carta*
October 12, 1492	*—*	*Columbus landed in the New World*
July 4, 1776	*Independence Day*	*The United States declared independence*
July 20, 1969	*—*	*Neil Armstrong set foot on the moon*

• **LESSON 90** • • • • • • • • • • • • • • • • • •

Seasons

Use of "I"

Copywork: "In the spring I…"

Poem review: "Mr. Nobody" (Lesson 81)

Note to Instructor: *Both the instructor and the student will need a pencil and paper.*

Continue to review "Mr. Nobody."

Instructor: Do you remember the four seasons: winter, spring, summer, and fall? What months are the coldest months—the winter months?

Student: *The winter months are December, January, and February.*

Instructor: What do you do in winter? Do you celebrate any holidays? How is the weather different from spring and summer?

Student: *In the winter I…*

Note to Instructor: *Help the student to answer these questions, if necessary. Remember that answers should be in complete sentences.*

Instructor: After the winter comes spring. The weather begins to be warmer. What months are the months of spring? (You may have to start the year for the student, "January, February…")

Student: *The spring months are March, April, and May.*

Instructor: What happens to trees and flowers in spring? What did the trees look like before spring? What flowers do you enjoy looking at? What is spring weather like?

Student: *In the spring…*

Instructor: After spring comes summer. What months are the months of summer? (Start naming the months of the year—January, February, March, April, May…)

Student: *The summer months are June, July, and September.*

Instructor: What is your favorite thing about summer? Do you have special company? Do you take a trip? Where do you go to cool off?

Note to Instructor: *If going to the pool, lake, or beach is an activity the student may actually do in summer, suggest that the student use some of the following list of words to give him ideas: sprinkler, water, pool, lake, boat, fish, beach, shells, sand, ocean.*

Student: *My favorite thing about summer is…*

Instructor: After winter, spring, and summer comes fall. What are the fall months?

Note to Instructor: *Prompt the student by beginning to name the months of the year: January, February, March, April, May, June, July, August...*

Student: *The fall months are September, October, November.*

Instructor: What do you see happening in fall? Do the leaves on the trees change color? Is the weather as hot as it was in summer? What holidays do you celebrate in fall?

Student: *In the fall I...*

Note to Instructor: *Write out one of the "I" statements that the student made in describing the seasons.*

Copywork

Ask the student to copy the "I" statement which you wrote out for him. Remind him that the pronoun "I" is always capitalized.

Enrichment Activity

Ask the student to write four "I" statements, one about each season. The statements should follow the pattern, "In the [season], I like to..."

· · · · · · · · · · · · · · · · · · LESSON 91 · · · · · · · · · · · · · ·

Story-poem narration: "Sunflowers"
Poem review: "Hearts Are Like Doors" (Lesson 27)

Notes to Instructor: *The instructor will need scissors and either a pencil and paper or a photocopy of the poem for the enrichment activity.*

Review "Hearts Are Like Doors" today.

Read "Sunflowers" aloud to the student and then have the student tell it back to you. The purpose of this exercise is to retell the sentences in the proper order. As necessary, use the questions following the poem to guide his recall of the sequence.

Sunflowers
Jessie Wise

Ben planted sunflower seeds.
The rain fell.
The sun warmed the soil.
Ben waited two weeks.
The seeds sprouted.
One plant grew huge leaves.
A big bud formed on the stem.
A gigantic flower opened.

Instructor: Who planted?
Student: *Ben planted.*

Instructor: What did he plant?
Student: *He planted sunflower seeds.*

Instructor: What two things were needed before the seeds sprouted?
Student: *The seeds needed sunlight and rain to sprout.*

Instructor: Did they sprout right away?
Student: *No, it took a while for the seeds to sprout.*

Instructor: How long did Ben have to wait for the seeds to sprout?
Student: *Ben waited two weeks.*

Instructor: After the plant sprouted, tell three things that the plant grew.
Student: *The plant grew leaves, a bud, and a flower.*

Instructor: Which grew first?
Student: *The leaves grew first.*

Instructor: Which grew second?
Student: *The bud grew second.*

Instructor: Which grew third?
Student: *The flower opened third.*

Enrichment Activity

Photocopy or write out the sentences. Cut them apart and have the student put them back into order again.

Introducing sentences
Copywork: "Practice makes perfect"
Poem review: "Mr. Nobody" (Lesson 81)

Note to Instructor: *The student will need a pencil and paper.*

Continue to review "Mr. Nobody."

Instructor: Today we are going to begin to learn about **sentences**. I will say the definition of a sentence for you three times. **A sentence is a group of words that expresses a complete thought.**

Note to Instructor: *Repeat three times.*

Instructor: Now let's say that definition together three times.

TOGETHER (three times): **A sentence is a group of words that expresses a complete thought.**

Instructor: A sentence begins with a capital letter and ends with a punctuation mark. Let's look at the sentences from the last lesson. Can you show me the capital letter at the beginning of each sentence? Can you show me the punctuation mark at the end of each sentence?

Ben planted sunflower seeds.

The rain fell.

The sun warmed the soil.

Ben waited two weeks.

The seeds sprouted.

One plant grew huge leaves.

A big bud formed on the stem.

A gigantic flower opened.

Instructor: **A sentence is a group of words that expresses a complete thought.** Listen to the difference between these two groups of words.

Ben planted sunflower seeds.
Sunflower seeds.

Which group of words expresses a complete thought? The first one. The second group of words is a fragment, not a sentence! A fragment means a piece of something. I will read you several groups of words. Listen to each, and tell me which group of words is a sentence and which is not.

One plant grew huge leaves. (sentence)
Grew huge leaves. (fragment)

The dinosaurs roamed over the land. (sentence)
The dinosaurs. (fragment)

Children on the soccer field. (fragment)
Children on the soccer field whooped for joy. (sentence)

Chocolate candy is the. (fragment)
Chocolate candy is the best dessert of all. (sentence)

Copywork

Choose one of the following sentences for the student to copy. After he has finished, ask him to show you the capital letter and the ending punctuation mark.

Practice makes perfect.

Do to others as you would have them do to you.

Never leave for tomorrow what you can do today.

········· **LESSON 93** ·················

Introducing sentence type 1: Statements

Note to Instructor: *The student will need a pencil and paper for the enrichment activity.*

Instructor: Listen to the definition of a sentence. **A sentence is a group of words that expresses a complete thought.** Let's say that together three times.

TOGETHER (three times): **A sentence is a group of words that expresses a complete thought.**

Instructor: All sentences begin with a capital letter and end with a punctuation mark. There are four different types of sentences. Today, we are going to talk about the first type of sentence—statements.

Statements tell you something. Statements give information. They end with a period. Here are several statements that tell you something and give you information.

The wind blows.
The girl skates.
The dogs run.
Trees have green leaves.
Cement is hard.

Now let's look back at the sentences in "Sunflowers" (Lesson 91). Each one of these sentences is a statement. Each statement tells us something about Ben or about the sunflowers. Point to the capital letter at the beginning of each statement. Now show me the period at the end.

Note to Instructor: *Ask the student to make five statements about people or objects he can see in the room where he is sitting. Make sure that these are complete sentences that give information.*

Enrichment Activity

Ask the student to make a statement giving information about a member of your family. He will begin the statement with the person's name. Then ask him to make a statement about himself, beginning with "I." He may write these statements, remembering to begin each statement with a capital letter and to end each statement with a period.

•••••••••••••••••••••   **LESSON 94**   •••••••••••••••••••

Introducing sentence type 2: Commands
Copywork: "Fried octopus"
Poem review: "Days of the Week" (Lesson 35)

Note to Instructor: *The student will need a pencil and paper.*

Review "Days of the Week" today.

Instructor: Now let's say the definition of a sentence together.

TOGETHER: **A sentence is a group of words that expresses a complete thought.**

Instructor: All sentences begin with a capital letter and end with a punctuation mark. Let's say that together three times.

TOGETHER (three times): All sentences begin with a capital letter and end with a punctuation mark.

Instructor: In the previous lesson we talked about the first type of sentence: the statement. Statements give information. Let's repeat that together three times: Statements give information.

TOGETHER (three times): Statements give information.

Instructor: Can you make a statement about yourself? Begin with "I am…"
Student: *I am… [a boy, a girl, hungry, thirsty, etc.].*

Instructor: There are four types of sentences. Today I am going to tell you about the second type of sentence: The command. Commands give an order or make a request. Let's say that together three times.

TOGETHER (three times): Commands give an order or make a request.

Instructor: Commands usually end with a period. I am going to give you some commands or requests:

Pick up your book.
Stand up.
Come here.

Other commands or requests you have heard are:

Come to breakfast.

Eat your supper.
Put your books away.
Pick up your toys.

Now it is your turn to give me some commands!

Note to Instructor: *Allow the student to give you reasonable commands. You may want to lay some ground rules first!*

Instructor: Now we have learned about two types of sentences. Statements give information. Commands give an order or make a request.

Copywork

According to the student's ability, choose one to three of these commands and have the student copy them. Remind the student that commands begin with capital letters and usually end with a period.

Eat neatly.

Do not eat with your toes.

Wipe your mouth after eating the fried octopus.

Enrichment Activity

Make a game of having the student give requests and commands to different members of the family. Silly, fun requests and commands are allowed if they are possible. If the student is writing easily, have him list these on paper. He may title the paper "Requests and Commands."

•••••••••••••••••••••• **LESSON 95** ••••••••••••••••••••

Introducing sentence type 3: Questions
Copywork: "Smaller than an elephant"

Note to Instructor: *Both the instructor and the student will need a pencil and paper. Also, in preparation for the lesson, consult your penmanship curriculum for the style of the question mark, which can differ from program to program.*

Instructor: Let's say the definition of a **sentence** together.

TOGETHER: **A sentence is a group of words that expresses a complete thought.**

Instructor: All sentences begin with a capital letter and end with a punctuation mark. Now let's say that together.

TOGETHER: All sentences begin with a capital letter and end with a punctuation mark.

Instructor: We have talked about sentences that are statements and sentences that are commands. Which type of sentence gives information?

Student: *A statement gives information.*

Instructor: Which type of sentence gives an order or makes a request?

Student: *A command gives an order or makes a request.*

Instructor: Today we are going to talk about a third type of sentence. A sentence that asks something is called a question. It ends with a question mark. Now I am going to ask you some questions. I'll ask the question and you answer the question in a complete sentence.

Instructor: What is your name?

Student *My name is _____.*

Instructor: You just answered my question with a statement. You gave me information. Now I will ask you another question. What is your favorite food?

Student: *My favorite food is _____.*

Instructor: What type of sentence did you just use?

Student: *I just used a statement.*

Instructor: Now you may ask me a question.

Note to Instructor: *Answer in a complete sentence! Point out that you have used a statement to answer a question.*

Instructor: What type of sentence is this? "Tell me your birthday."

Student: *That is a command.*

Instructor: What type of sentence is "When is your birthday?"

Student: *That is a question.*

Instructor: Now you know three different types of sentences. A statement gives information. A command gives an order or makes a request. And a question asks something. The answers to questions are usually statements. What punctuation mark comes at the end of a statement or command?

Student: *Statements and commands end with periods.*

Instructor: What punctuation mark comes at the end of a question?

Student: *A question mark comes at the end of a question.*

Instructor: I will show you how to make a question mark. Then I want you to practice making five question marks on your own paper.

Copywork

According to the student's ability, choose one to three of the following questions.

How much do you weigh?

Are you bigger than a kangaroo?

Are you bigger than a dog and smaller than an elephant?

Enrichment Activity

Play the commands and questions game "May I?" The instructor gives a command such as "Stand up," then follows with possible commands such as "Pick up your pencil," "Come here," "Turn around," "Pick up one foot," "Put your foot down," etc. Before the student obeys the command, he must say, "May I?" If he fails to ask "May I?" he must sit down where he is until told to stand up again.

· · · · · · · · · · · · · · · · · · ·   **LESSON 96**   · · · · · · · · · · · · · · · · ·

Introducing sentence type 4: Exclamations
Copywork: "The pig is radiant!"

Note to Instructor: *Both the instructor and the student will need a pencil and paper.*

Instructor: Now, we have talked about three types of sentences. Statements give us information. Commands give an order or make a request. Questions ask something. What does a question do?

Student: *A question asks something.*

Instructor: What does a command do?

Student: *A command gives an order or makes a request.*

Instructor: What does a statement do?

Student: *A statement gives information.*

Instructor: The fourth type of sentence is called an exclamation. An exclamation shows sudden or strong feeling. It ends with an exclamation point. Some sudden or strong feelings are excitement, surprise, fear, and anger. Here are some exclamations that show strong feeling and end with exclamation points.

Note to Instructor: *When reading exclamatory sentences, speak louder and use lots of expression!*

Instructor: I won!
Ouch, I touched that hot stove!
Help, I can't swim!
The sink is running over!
Watch out for the giant pink alien!
There is a twelve-legged spider on your head!

Instructor: I am going to make a statement. "A pig with wings just flew by the window." Can you make that into a question?

Student: *Did a pig with wings just fly by the window?*

Instructor: Now can you make that into an exclamation?

Student: *A pig with wings just flew by the window!*

Instructor: "Look at the pig with wings." What type of sentence is that?

Student: *That is a command.*

Instructor: I am going to make an exclamation point for you. Then, you make a line of ten neat exclamation points on your own paper.

Copywork

Ask the student to copy one to three of the following sentences. Remind him to begin each sentence with a capital letter and end it with an exclamation point.

The pig is radiant!

The radiant pig is doing a backflip!

That spider just wove words into her web!

Enrichment Activity

Let the student read the exclamatory sentences above, speaking loudly and using lots of expression!

Four types of sentences

Note to Instructor: *The student may need a pencil and paper for the enrichment activity.*

Instructor: Remember, all sentences begin with capital letters and end with punctuation marks. As we read the sentences below about a sunflower garden, I want you to point to the capital letter at the beginning of each sentence and say, "All sentences begin with a capital letter." We will read the sentences together. When we have finished reading the sentence, tell me what mark of punctuation is at the end of each, and what type of sentence it is.

Note to Instructor: *If the student cannot yet read these sentences, read them aloud while moving your finger beneath the words. When necessary, guide the student by asking questions.*

Instructor: Please read the sentence below.

Ben planted sunflower seeds.

Instructor: What kind of letter begins all sentences?
Student [pointing to beginning of sentence]: All sentences begin with a capital letter.

Instructor: What type of sentence is this?
Student: *This sentence is a statement.*

Instructor: A statement ends with what kind of punctuation mark?
Student [pointing to end of sentence]: A statement ends with a period.

Instructor: Please read the sentence below.

Do not step where I planted seeds.

Instructor: What kind of letter begins all sentences?
Student [pointing to beginning of sentence]: All sentences begin with a capital letter.

Instructor: This sentence isn't a statement. What does this sentence do?
Student: *This sentence gives an order or a makes a request.*

Instructor: This sentence is a command. With what kind of punctuation mark does a command or a request usually end?
Student: *A command or a request usually ends with a period.*

Instructor: Please read the sentence below.

    When will the sunflowers ever come up?

Instructor: What kind of letter begins all sentences?
Student [pointing to beginning of sentence]: All sentences begin with a capital letter.

Instructor: What type of sentence is this?
Student: *This sentence is a question.*

Instructor: With what kind of punctuation mark does a question end?
Student: *A question ends with a question mark.*

Instructor: Please read the sentence below.

    Wow! My sunflower is huge!

Instructor: What kind of letter begins all sentences?
Student [pointing to beginning of sentence]: All sentences begin with a capital letter.

Instructor: What type of sentence is this?
Student: *This sentence is an exclamation.*

Instructor: What does an exclamation do?
Student: *An exclamation shows sudden or strong feeling.*

Instructor: With what punctuation mark does an exclamation end?
Student: *An exclamation ends with an exclamation point.*

Enrichment Activity

Have the student make up one of each type of sentence. If he is writing easily, he should write the sentence with correct capitalization and punctuation.

•   **LESSON 98**   • • • • • • • • • • • • • • • • • •

Nouns
Types of sentences
Verbs

Instructor: Let's say the definition of a noun together.

TOGETHER: **A noun is the name of a person, place, thing, or idea.**

Instructor: Can you make a statement about a person in this room?
Student: *[statement]*

Instructor: Can you ask a question about a place you would like to visit?
Student: *[question]*

Instructor: Can you give me a command? Tell me what to do with a thing in this room.
Student :   *[command]*

Instructor: Finally, make a strong exclamation about an idea—a feeling such as joy, surprise, happiness, or fear.
Student: *[exclamation]*

Instructor: I am going to say the definition of a verb three times for you.

Instructor (three times): **A verb is a word that does an action, shows a state of being, links two words together, or helps another verb.**

Instructor: Now I want you to repeat parts of this definition after me: **A verb is a word that does an action.**
Student: *A verb is a word that does an action.*

Instructor: Now listen to the second part of the definition: **Shows a state of being.** Repeat that for me.
Student: *Shows a state of being.*

Instructor: **Links two words together.**
Student: *Links two words together.*

Instructor: **Or helps another verb.**
Student: *Or helps another verb.*

Instructor: Now you have learned all about nouns and verbs—and about the four types of sentences that use them! I think that you should run around and do some action verbs instead of doing copywork today!

••••••••••••••••••• **LESSON 99** •••••••••••••••••••

Cumulative poem review

Instructor: Today we are going to review all of the poems you have worked on so far. When we recite a poem, we begin with the title and author. I will read each poem to you, and then I want you to try to say the poem back to me. Remember: Stand up straight! Don't fidget while you're reciting! And speak in a nice, loud, slow voice.

Note to Instructor: *Read each poem to the student before asking him to repeat it. If he repeats it accurately, move on to the next poem. If he stumbles, ask him to repeat the line he cannot remember three times, and make a note to review that poem daily until it is mastered. Remind the student that "Anonymous" means we don't know who wrote the poem.*

Lesson	Poem	Author
2	"The Caterpillar"	Christina G. Rossetti
15	"Work"	Anonymous
27	"Hearts Are Like Doors"	Anonymous
35	"Days of the Week"	Mother Goose rhyme, adapted by Sara Buffington
43	"The Months"	Mother Goose rhyme
81	"Mr. Nobody"	Anonymous

•••••••••••••••••••• **LESSON 100** •••••••••••••••••••

Identifying sentences in "The Goops"

Instructor: For this lesson, I am going to read you a poem about the Goops. Can you find an exclamation in this poem? Can you find a question? Can you find a statement?

Note to Instructor: *Because this is cast into poetic form, you should consider each line to be a separate sentence, with the exception of the last two lines; "And that is why I'm glad that I am not a Goop" is one sentence, while "Are you?" is a separate sentence. "Oh, they lead disgusting lives!" is an exclamation. "Are you?" is a question. The other lines in the poem are statements.*

The Goops
Gelett Burgess

The Goops they lick their fingers,
And the Goops they lick their knives,
They spill their broth on the tablecloth-
Oh, they lead disgusting lives!
The Goops they talk while eating,
And loud and fast they chew,
And that is why I'm glad that I
Am not a Goop - are you?

Note to Instructor: *The second level of* First Language Lessons *begins with memorization of "The Goops," providing the student with continuity.*

·············· **FINAL GRAMMAR REVIEW** ··············

Instructor: Today we are going to review the grammar that we've learned this year! Let's start with nouns. What is a noun?

Student: *A noun is the name of a person, place, thing, or idea.*

Instructor: Can you tell me a common noun that names a person?

Student: *[Girl, boy, mother, father]*

Instructor: Can you tell me a common noun that names a place?

Student: *[Store, library, zoo, park]*

Instructor: Can you tell me a proper noun that names a person?

Student: *[Name]*

Instructor: The name of your street, your city, and your state are all proper nouns that name places. Recite your address for me.

Student: *[Address]*

Instructor: Now tell me some nouns that name living things.

Student: *[Bee, shark, potato, pecan, rose, cat]*

Instructor: The days of the week are proper nouns. Can you tell me the days of the week in order, beginning with Sunday?

Student: *Sunday, Monday, Tuesday, Wednesday, Thursday, Friday, Saturday*

Instructor: What is a pronoun?

Student: *A pronoun is a word used in the place of a noun.*

Instructor: You have learned lists of pronouns that take the place of nouns. Recite them for me, beginning with "I, me, my, mine."

Student: *I, me, my, mine; you, your, yours; he, she, him, her, it, his, hers, its; we, us, our, ours; they, them, their, theirs.*

Instructor: Fish swim in the water. What pronoun can you use in place of "fish"?

Student: *They*

Instructor: A boy sits on a wall. What prounoun can you use in place of "boy"?

Student: *He*

Instructor: [Instructor's name] and [student's name] are doing grammar. What pronoun can you use in place of "[instructor's name] and [student's name]"?

Student:	*We*

Instructor:	What is a verb?
Student:	*A verb is a word that does an action, shows a state of being, links two words together, or helps another verb.*

Instructor:	In the sentence "The girl dances," which word is the action verb?
Student:	*Dances*

Instructor:	Can you recite the months of the year for me?
Student:	*January, February, March, April, May, June, July, August, September, October, November, December*

Instructor:	Those are proper nouns. The names of the seasons are not proper nouns, though. They are common nouns. Do you remember the names of the four seasons?
Student:	*Summer, fall, winter, spring*

Instructor:	What is a sentence?
Student:	*A sentence is a group of words that expresses a complete thought.*

Instructor:	What does a sentence begin with?
Student:	*A sentence begins with a capital letter.*

Instructor:	What does a sentence end with?
Student:	*A sentence ends with a punctuation mark.*

Instructor:	There are four kinds of sentences. What do statements do?
Student:	*Statements give information.*

Instructor:	What do commands do?
Student:	*Commands give an order or make a request.*

Instructor:	What is a sentence that asks something?
Student:	*A sentence that asks something is called a question.*

Instructor:	What does an exclamation do?
Student:	*An exclamation shows sudden or strong feeling.*

Instructor:	You have learned so much grammar this year! That is an exclamation. It shows strong feeling. I feel strongly that you have done a wonderful job learning grammar!

Glossary of Terms and Definitions

Terms

action verb—An action verb is a word that does an action.

command—A command gives an order or makes a request.

common noun—A common noun is the name of any person, place, thing, or idea.

exclamation—An exclamation shows sudden or strong feeling.

noun—A noun is the name of a person, place, thing, or idea.

pronoun—A pronoun is a word used in place of a noun.

proper noun—A proper noun is a word that names a particular person, place, thing, or idea.

question—A question asks something.

sentence—A sentence is a group of words that expresses a complete thought.

statement—A statement gives information.

verb—A verb is a word that does an action, shows a state of being, links two words together, or helps another verb.

Memorized Definitions

A noun is the name of a person, place, thing, or idea.

A pronoun is a word used in place of a noun.

A verb is a word that does an action, shows a state of being, links two words together, or helps another verb.

A sentence is a group of words that expresses a complete thought.

Memorized Lists

Pronouns:

I, me, my, mine;

you, your, yours;

he, she, him, her, it, his, hers, its;

we, us, our, ours;

they, them, their, theirs.

Poems

Index